Things I Want to Tell You

BEFORE I DROP DEAD

LOUIS ROMANO

Published by Vecchia.

Vecchia Publishing, 41 Grand Avenue, Suite 101, River Edge, New Jersey, 07661

ISBN: 978-1-944906-24-5

Printed in the U.S.A. First Edition, 2019 Vecchia Publishing

Also by Louis Romano

Detective Vic Gonnella Series
INTERCESSION
YOU THINK I'M DEAD
JUSTIFIED
THE BUTCHER OF PUNTA CANA

Gino Ranno Mafia Series
FISH FARM
BESA
GAME OF PAWNS
EXCLUSION: THE FIGHT FOR CHINATOWN

Zip Code Series for Teens & Young Adults
ZIP CODE

Short Story & Poetry Series
Anxiety's Nest
Anxiety's Cure

Heritage Collection Series
CARUSI: The Shame of Sicily

Acknowledgments & Dedication

I would like to thank every person I ever hung out with as a kid growing up in the Bronx. My childhood gives me some vivid memories. These stories and poems are my interpretation of some real events in my life, then and now.

There are so many, it's difficult to thank all the people who influenced me as a Bronx teenager back in the 1960s and as a young adult in New Jersey to where I have now been exiled.

If any of my old friends or family are around and are still talking to me, they know who they are and need no special nod. Our friendship and conversation always picks up where it left off.

My later in life friends and acquaintances who inspired some of these stories are, cigar buddies, Allan "Freddie" Erps, Barry Werk, Mark Allen, Larry Pirone (back cover photo credit!), and Bronx guys Eugene Duffy and Ian Lowell.

Special thanks must go out, though, to the duo of Bridget Fuchsel and Kathleen Collins, without whom this book would never make it to print.

And of course thanks to every member of my family and Rocco the dog who just celebrated his 13th birthday.

TABLE OF CONTENTS

PABLO

At seven years old, I had no born or learned prejudices, so making a new friend had no barriers.

The boy looked to be about my age. He was chubby, with a great, wide smile and round face that betrayed his excitement at being in a new home, basically another world.

It was the summer of 1958 when the first families of Puerto Ricans started moving into the tenement houses on Clinton Avenue in the Bronx; the neighborhood was not at all prepared for the influx of this different culture.

Mostly Italian, Jewish, Irish, and German, the most crime the block experienced was the occasional and impromptu dice games. Some of the knock-around guys would play for money in the gutter between the few parked cars which were used to mask the game from the cops.

The Puerto Ricans were so unknown that the word 'spic' was not yet even in the daily parlance.

I was playing with my marbles, which were in a Bering Cigar box when he ran up to me and looked into the box at the multi-colored, round pieces of glass.

"¡Hola!," He said.

"Marbles…do you have some?" I replied.

The happy boy gave me a quizzical look. I realized he didn't speak English, but that was ok. I knew plenty of Italian kids who didn't speak my language so there was always just a lot of gesturing going on and a few words to help us communicate.

"What's your name?" I uttered anyway.

"¿Que?"

I pointed to myself.

"I'm Louis."

"Ah...Luis... Pablo," he said pointing to himself.

I handed Pablo a few marbles and we both sat on the concrete walkway in front of my stoop at 2076 Clinton Avenue. My mother's boundaries were the walkway between the adjoining building on the right side and Johnny Fader's tiny grocery store on the left. My entire frontier was less than twenty-five yards.

I emptied the marbles onto the pavement and put the cigar box down with its open side facing the ground. The holes my dad made for me on the side of the box were the targets to shoot the marbles into. Pablo caught on fast.

We played for a while and Pablo finally spoke.

"¿Mootato chiefs?" Pablo asked.

"What?"

"Mootato chiefs," Pablo repeated.

I shrugged my shoulders not knowing what he meant and shot my steely into the hole.

Pablo gave me a hand gesture to just wait right there and he jumped up and ran to his building. He was wearing brown sandals. I'd never seen a boy who wore sandals before. All of the kids I knew wore P.F. Flyers or Ked sneakers. As a matter of fact, the only time I ever saw anyone wearing sandals were when the Franciscan monks were visiting the church, and they had them on under their long, brown robes.

A few minutes later, Pablo ran back with a folded, terry cloth kitchen towel.

He sat down next to me and slowly unfolded his towel.

"Mootato chiefs…mmmm goot."

Golden brown, homemade potato chips were in the towel."Oh… potato chips!" I blurted.

"Si, mootato chiefs."

Pablo offered the chips to me, both of us munching on the fried, salted buds. They may have been the best mootato chiefs I ever had.

"Baseboll?"

"Yes, I like baseball," I answered.

"Jankees?"

"Yes…the Yankees. Everyone in the Bronx likes the Yankees."

"Mickey Mantle. Jogi Berra."

"Yes, and Whitey Ford, too."

"Jes, Whitey Ford e el Moose," Pablo yelled. He was referring to Bill 'Moose' Skowron, the Yankee first baseman."

'Yes, the Moose!"

"Mickey Mantle…hong run!" Pablo waved his arms as if he was hitting the ball out of the park.

We were finding common ground and becoming fast friends, neither of us speaking the same language.

Pablo was a nice kid. I could see our future: He would learn English, and maybe I would learn his language along the way.

Shortly thereafter, an old Chevy pulled onto Clinton Avenue. The driver waved at Pablo and beeped the horn. Pablo's mother and a few other older people were coming out of their building. They were carrying blankets and a picnic basket and some brown paper bags that looked like they were filled with something.

Pablo's mother called to him. I couldn't understand what she was saying, but Pablo explained their plans.

"Vamos, al lago a nadir," his mom yelled.

Again, I shrugged my shoulders, my face explaining I didn't understand what she was saying.

Pablo mimed swimming, and off he went, running toward the car and his family.

"Ah, okay…okay!"

"Bye-bye, Luis."

"See ya, Pablo."

Part of me wished I was going with them but I knew that wasn't happening. Anyway, my mother was getting ready to take my little brother and me to the Bronx Zoo. It was a free admission day and we would meet up with my aunt and cousins. Mom had a picnic of her own planned for us.

We arrived at the zoo just in time to see the seals being fed in their water enclosure. While the seals barked for more fish, the lions were also being fed in the next caged enclosure, roaring their approval.

Mom pushed my brother in his stroller and we walked until I was so tired and hot I almost asked to jump into the stroller. I was a big boy now, though, so I didn't.

We all walked the six or seven blocks back to Clinton Avenue. It had been another great day being with my cousins and seeing the animals, and I couldn't wait to mimic them to Pablo when he returned from his own outing. I laughed to myself thinking of how I was going to imitate the low-land gorillas who were my all-time favorite because they would sometimes throw their fruit peels and their feces at the crowd. Today they didn't disappoint and we all ducked from their excrement. My mom and aunt screamed and the kids all laughed in hysterics.

At five-thirty my father would be coming home from work and my mom had our supper all ready for us on the stove. I decided to go down to wait for my father, meeting him as he walked from the bus stop on 180th Street.

As my dad walked, he waved to me, and I waved back. I was smiling myself when I saw the happy boy's car that took Pablo and his family to swim coming down Clinton Avenue. I looked into the Chevy for my new friend, but I didn't see him.

Dad and I reached our building and were starting to walk up the steps of the stoop when we heard a blood curdling scream. It was Pablo's mother. Two of the men held her under her arms as she walked toward their building.

"¡Ay dios, mio…ay dios, mio…Pablo es mort!" she screamed.

"What the hell happened?" Dad asked to no one.

Dad and I turned back and walked toward the pandemonium outside Pablo's building. "What's happening, dad?" I asked. My dad put his hand on my shoulder stopping me from walking any closer as an older woman came out of the building, for she, too, was crying and screaming hysterically at the news. "Dad!" I said starting to panic, but not knowing why.

"¡No…por favor, Dios…No, Pablo!" the older woman howled. She ran to Pablo's mother hugging her hard and both women collapsed to the concrete pavement.

"Jesus Christ, Almighty…her kid is dead," Dad said. He understood what they were saying as it is close to Italian.

"What? Her kid? Pablo?" I asked.

Dad told me to stay put as he went and spoke to one of the men from the car. He was able to find out Pablo had drowned at the lake up in New York State.

"¡Ay dios, mio…Pablo es mort!" another woman in the crowd shrieked.

I was stunned. I would never get to see that chubby kid again. We would never get to know each other. No baseball, marbles, stickball, nothing. He would never learn English and I would never again taste his mother's 'mootato chiefs'.

I didn't cry. I guess I didn't know him well enough to cry and have a great sense of loss. I guess at seven years old I didn't know how to cry about death yet. Now I do.

MRS. HALPER

The second-floor window was manned all day, every day, by Jenny Halper. Her enormous size filled the frame, her billowing white hair, pale-white wrinkled complexion and toothless smile watched the neighborhood better than Uncle John the beat cop, who twirled his nightstick in sync with his slow stroll.

It was the mid 1950s in The Bronx, when the beat cop didn't have a single arrest for the ten years he walked the streets.

Every day, rain or shine, Mrs. Halper's brother Jake came to visit at ten to nine in the morning. He sat in a blanket covered soft chair watching every game show and soap opera on the twelve inch Andrea black and white television. He especially liked The Liberace Show, and the fifteen-minute music show with the famed Nat 'King' Cole. With a break for lunch and a nosh or three, then supper and the regular evening shows, Jake would leave promptly at eleven-fifteen when CBS Channel 2 news would end. Jake sat in the dark, the only light emanated from the T.V.

Mrs. Halper moved slowly. She walked from the kitchen down a small hallway to the bathroom and through the small living room where her brother sat all day. Through double French glass doors into her bedroom and to her guardian station at the window facing Clinton Avenue she sat. Her enormous weight actually touched both sides of the hallway as she waddled down it. Mrs. Halper never left the apartment, a veritable shut-in. There was no way she could fit into the small porcelain tub that took up most of the bathroom. Sponge baths in her bed was the only way she could possibly clean her massive body.

Late one morning, Mrs. Halper, was smiling down at me from the double-wide window as she always did, watching that I was safe. I was all of five years old. She called to me with a raspy voice that was just above a whisper.

"Louis, bubbala, come up by Mrs. Halper."

Dutifully, I ran up the five black slate stoop steps and into the vestibule, up three marble steps, down the dingy hallway over the black and white tiled floor, and up two flights of worn steps to Mrs. Halper's apartment.

It was summertime so the front door was wide open. Leaving the door open and the open window where Mrs. Halper sat, gave a cross ventilation through the apartment. That was the nineteen-fifties rendition of air conditioning,

I ran past Jake toward the bedroom where Mrs. Halper sat. I don't recall if Jake even noticed my speedy entrance.

"Louis, go into my purse and take two dollars." It was Saturday so Mrs. Halper refrained from touching money. It was my first duty at being a Shabbos goy.

She produced a small paper bag with the wrappings from various food items. Grossinger's rye bread, Mueller's Muenster cheese, the label of a Manischewitz borscht bottle, and a crumpled label off a can of Moosabec skinless and boneless sardines. She explained that fish and dairy was kosher, as if I knew what keeping Kosher was all about.

"Louis, go around the corner to the deli and hand Morris this bag. He will put the change in the bag. Bring the bag back by me boychick. Careful not to drop it," Mrs. Halper uttered. Her perennial smile never changed.

I ran quickly by Jake and I heard the announcer say, "As the World Turns," on the Andrea. I pictured the world turning like the small globe my parents had on a shelf in our living-room.

Down all the steps, I never broke my stride until I entered the deli where I kicked the light brown sawdust on the floor all the way to the counter.

Morris filled the order, not saying a word, closing the bag with a folded crumble."Don't drop this or the glass will break. Walk, don't run boychick. Jenny's change is inside," Morris stated. He was less religious than Mrs. Halper so Morris opened his store every day.

I held the bag with both hands and walked back to Mrs. Halper. I passed a puddle in the street that was called 'pollo water' and I noticed a swarm of mosquitoes hovering above the black water. I almost ran from that puddle but remembered that I was carrying glass and headed Morris' admonition to walk.

I headed carefully and slowly up the stairs and back into Mrs. Halper's apartment where she was waiting in her kitchen for my return. It likely took her that much time to get from the window to the linoleum floored kitchen where she sat on a chair, one of four that surrounded the table. Most of Mrs. Halper hung off either side of the chair as she caught her breath from the effort it took her to walk through the apartment.

"Thank you, Louis. Would you turn the light on for Mrs. Halper?"

I flipped the switch illuminating the tiny kitchen not knowing that this was also part of the Shabbos goy's job.

Mrs. Halper opened the paper bag and took each item out like they were precious, placing them gently onto the table. She took a nickel from the change in the bag and handed the coin to me.

"Thank you, Louis. Here take this and get some candy."

I looked at the buffalo on the coin and closed it tightly into my hand.

"Jacob, come in for some lunch," Mrs. Halper called out to her brother as I ran back down the stairway onto the steamy concrete pavement.

I walked to the outer edge of my boundary, the corner of 180th Street and Clinton Avenue. Candy was out of the question as I couldn't cross the street to Jerry Bush's candy store. But, here was this nickel burning a hole into my palm. On the corner of my block was a Jewish delicatessen with a pickle barrel outside. The wooden barrel was covered with a plastic top, the fat pickles floating in the brine. The aroma was awesome.

I walked inside the store and was immediately overtaken by the delicious aroma of grilled hot dogs, sauerkraut, and steaming pastrami. I slapped the nickel on the worn, white counter and asked the counter man for a pickle.

"A pickle for a nickel," he pronounced as he walked around the counter with a sheet of waxed paper in one hand and a long fork in the other.

My mouth was watering as the counter man removed the top of the barrel.

"Let's see. Let's get the fattest one we can find. How about this one?" He pointed his fork at an enormous floater which met my approval.

Wrapped in the wax paper, I walked down the street with the hard-earned pickle. The first bite snapped in my mouth with a salty-briny explosion that made my lips pucker and my eyes tear. I devoured the transformed cucumber, its juice running down my hand onto my arm and tee shirt.

Crumpling the wax paper and putting it into the pocket of my shorts I suddenly needed something cold to drink. I ran home.

Our apartment was directly across from Mrs. Halper's. I bounded up the stairs and ran into my mother's kitchen. Mom always kept a plastic pitcher of water in the fridge so I grabbed a glass that once held Welch's grape jelly, and over filled it, spilling the icy water on the kitchen table.

Mom entered the kitchen.

"LOUIS!!! Look at the mess you're making!" she screeched. "Jesus, Mary, and Joseph! And what is that smell? You reek of garlic. Where have you been?"

"I had a pickle."

"A pickle? How did you get a pickle?"

"I went to the store for Mrs. Halper and she gave me a nickel. A nickel for a pickle!" I parroted the counter man's quote.

Mom cuffed me on the side of my head spilling more of the water from the glass that was in my hand.

"You took money from that woman? What are you a street urchin? A beggar? That woman is a saint. She babysat your father. I've never been so embarrassed in my whole life." Mom had a flare for the dramatic.

Mom opened her purse and handed a nickel over. "Now you march right over and give this to Mrs. Halper and apologize for taking her money this instant."

I walked into Mrs. Halper's apartment my head down, wiping my eyes from the cuff my mom handed me.

Jake finally looked up from the television

"Jenny, the boy is back. He's upset!" Jake hollered.

The French doors were open so I walked into Mrs. Halper's bedroom.

"What? What? What's the matter, Louis?"

I started to cry again, this time feeling sorry for myself. I handed the nickel my mom gave me to Mrs. Halper.

"I'm not an urchin or an urching. I'm not even a beggar. I don't even know what that means. My mom said I can't take money from you anymore."

"Come, bubbala, come to the kitchen with Mrs. Halper. Let's have a little nosh. I'll have a talk with your mother about this the next time she pops in. For now, let's see what's in the fridge."

Mrs. Halper struggled to pull her weight from the cushioned chair. Holding onto the chair and then the bedpost and then another chair she walked, rocking from side to side through the living room, down the hallway and into the dark kitchen. I followed behind her and even at that young age I knew that her size was not a good thing. She was sucking in breath with every other step, emitting a wheezing sound which rattled off the faded paint plaster walls.

I flicked the lights on in the kitchen and Mrs. Halper sat to catch her breath; her constant smile had turned into a pained grimace.

She pointed to the refrigerator door and I opened it with some effort. It seemed older and heavier than the fridge my mom had. There was no light when I opened the door. My mom's fridge had a light inside.

Mrs. Halper pointed to a quart of milk and waved for me to take it and place it on the table. Then she waved to a dish which was covered with a sheet of shiny aluminum foil. She poured the milk into a white coffee cup that was stained inside. I wasn't crazy about drinking milk or anything else from a cup that was stained but I didn't want to say anything or refuse the drink.

Next, Mrs. Halper removed the foil from the plate exposing something that looked interesting to me. I never had potato pancakes before. She placed one pancake on a small white napkin for me and one for her.

She took a big, gummy bite out of the pancake, all the while her eyes smiling at me. I grabbed the fried delight and took a big bite like Mrs. Halper did. The taste of onion infused in the potato was sublime. I've never had a potato pancake since that was anywhere nearly as delicious. I vividly recall that moment with this wonderful, loving woman over sixty-years later.

After the pancakes there was chocolate rugelach, another food I never had before. Mrs. Halper encouraged me to dunk the rugelach into my milk. I completely forgot about the stain in the cup.

I saw Mrs. Halper every day of my life, either at the window or helping her with some small chore in her apartment.

On my way home from school one day about a year later I looked up at the second-floor window to see Mrs. Halper and wave to her.

This day the window was closed and the drapes were drawn. I ran up, taking two steps at a time. Mrs. Halper's apartment door was closed and Jake, my mom, and a few neighbors were standing in the hallway. Mom and her friend, Adie, Mrs. Halper's daughter-in-law, were hugging each other and crying. Jake stood there, his eyes were closed and his head bowed low. I knew Mrs. Halper was gone.

I overheard one of the neighbors say Mrs. Halper died in her sleep and it took five men to carry her down the stairs into the car that took her away.

The neighborhood was never the same while Mrs. Halper wasn't at her window. Another family took the apartment but I swear I felt Mrs. Halper's presence in that hallway every day.

We moved not too long after Jenny Halper died, maybe a year at most. The neighborhood was changing every day. Moving trucks taking furniture and boxes from the apartments on a daily basis. The new people who were moving in were very different than the people who were moving out.

I remember the blue moving truck, American Indian Head Movers, with all of our furniture and suitcases and boxes, pulling away from the front of the building, my father following in his car, me and my brother in the back seat. My mom holding my baby brother in her arms in the front seat. Mom was dabbing her eyes with a Kleenex tissue as we left.

I turned in my seat to look up at the second-floor window for the last time. I pretended that Mrs. Halper was waving and smiling down at us. I waved at the closed, empty window until the building was out of sight.

LOUIS BROWN

Memories are often defined by events and places that families pass on from generation to generation. Some families are devoted to sailing, a sports team, ski trips, religion, or a business. My grandfather, Louie Romano, a.k.a. Louie Brown, and my father, Joey, passed down a tradition that was seared into my memory from the time I could smell. That place was a restaurant which was owned by my dad's Uncle Bill, a.k.a. Bill Half Moon. There were lots of a.k.a.s in my life.

When Grandpa Louie told the story about the mob guy and his side girlfriend, he would captivate the room with his visual interpretation.

Because of You was playing on the table jukebox at The Half Moon restaurant on East 187th Street in the Bronx. The year was 1951, and Tony Bennett had had his first big hit.

Every one of the booths at this small, Neapolitan, pizzeria restaurant had the small jukebox with the classic hits of the day and some standard oldies like Darktown Strutters Ball that brought the customers to the romantic place they either longed for or imagined. A nickel a song, or seven for a quarter, fit in well with the menu pricing of the post-war boom era.

A beautifully thin, sliced, veal parmigiana with spaghetti dinner was a dollar twenty. A delightfully delicious, squat and straw-covered bottle of Martini and Rossi Chianti was eighty-five cents, and you got to keep the ornate little bottle for later use as a candle holder.

To put things in their proper perspective, a new house was under sixteen thousand dollars, and the average income was somewhere just above three thousand bucks a year.

The Half Moon had a unique aura that can best be described by using all of the senses simultaneously. The sounds of the music from the jukes, the rattling of dishes and glasses from the kitchen, welcoming, white, table-clothed tables, all under a fifteen foot wide, three foot tall, subtly dark oil painting of Mount Vesuvius smoking above a bay where fishermen tended to their boats and nets in a moonlit setting, hung above the bar. The charcoal brick oven emitted the delectable aroma of homemade dough that was transformed into thin crust pizza and plump ricotta and ham-filled calzones by a compact stump of a man, dressed in an all-white restaurant uniform, who we called Louie Pie. Louie's white hair and powerful, short arms threw the elastic pizza dough high into the air to the amazement of everyone who ever saw him perform his craft.

Everyone was greeted by their hands being shaken or their cheeks being kissed by their favorite waiter or bartender or friends at nearby tables. Finally, the incomparable taste of the food, that would make the diner roll their eyes in ecstasy and moan low with delight.

The pizza, made with crushed San Marzano tomatoes, crumbled fresh mozzarella cheese, finished with a swirl of olive oil, a pinch of fresh ground oregano, a sprinkling of parmigiano cheese, then dotted with basil leaves, was a literal work of art when it came out of the oven after two minutes. The pizza crust had huge dough bubbles from the seven hundred degree heat of the oven. The bottom of the pie was darkened by the oven's intensity with a one-of-a-kind charcoal taste.

There was an excitement about the Half Moon that took off like a jet every day at noon and came to a smooth landing at three o'clock the next morning.

On this particular September, Friday night, a made-man, who we will call Sally Glasses, came into the restaurant, like clockwork, at seven-thirty in the evening. His table was ready, the music in his romantic booth for two was playing his list of songs and his drink, a Rob-Roy on the rocks, was waiting at his place.

Sally Glasses kissed grandpa on both cheeks, and the sexy, young blonde with him, who had teased hair in a seemingly two-story high, beehive bun, kissed Louie Brown a bit too close to his mouth for grandpa's comfort.

Why this very handsome, quiet grandpa had a nickname was never spoken of or really explained, so we will leave it to the imagination.

Sally Glasses was a capo in the infamous Gambino crime family and at lunchtime, every so often, Sally came into the Half Moon for pasta Faggioli with Don Carlo Gambino. Don Carlo was unassuming in his zippered jacket and common fedora. No one would suspect that this man with the ample nose was the most powerful mafia boss in the entire United States.

Sally, on the other hand, was always nattily dressed in his black, sharkskin, pinstripe suit, silk socks, shiny, pointed shoes, an orange necktie, and matching orange pocket square.

The blonde ordered a Rye Presbyterian because it sounded sophisticated. Her form-fitting, green dress showed off her ample cleavage adorned with a gold and diamond necklace. She broke off the heel of the oven-toasted, Italian bread placed in a napkin-covered basket which was placed on the table by Grandpa Louie. She took out a Parliament cigarette and waited for Sally to look up from the menu. The mobster held up his gold and diamond-encrusted lighter. Blondie softly wrapped her hands around Sally's manicured hand as she gave him a sexy look and a comely wink before erotically blowing out the flame.

Sally Glasses ordered his usual muscles marinara fra diavolo appetizer and spaghetti with white clam sauce.

The young lady ordered veal parmigiana with linguine until Sally reminded her it was Friday. She went with clams on the half-shell and lobster tails. They shared a bottle of Chianti.

Grandpa Louie doted on the couple and served a small, Neapolitan, six-slice pizza pie with grated parmesan cheese as Sally liked, after the meal.

Sally had another Rob-Roy, while the bombshell polished off the rest of the bottle of red wine. They both had a demitasse with anisette, enjoyed with another cigarette each.

Glasses gave grandpa the writing sign for the check which was no more than eight dollars.

These were the days before credit cards, and Sally put the eight dollars in cash in the check billfold, leaving three singles on the table for Louie Brown.

Sally got up from the table, straightened out his suit jacket and tie as he waited for blondie to slink out of the booth, him catching a pretty good view of her luscious thighs as she moved.

As the dapper mob guy moved for the door, he realized that he left his cigarette lighter on the table. As he turned to retrieve the piece, he noticed that his girl had palmed one of the three dollars that were left for grandpa Louie.

"Go wait outside," Sally commanded.

Blondie wiggled her way out of the Half Moon's front door.

Sally Glasses' face went from pale to red in a second. He sat down at the table.

"Louie…do me a favor…sit down," Sally ordered, pointing to the blonde's seat. Grandpa Louie, knowing what was coming, obediently sat.

"Louie Brown, I know you a long time, so answer my question. How long is this broad doing this to you?"

"Aww, Sally, no big deal. Don't make a…" Grandpa tried.

"Listen to me, Louie. I axed you a question, now give me an answer," Sally steamed.

Grandpa threw the babe under the bus.

"Since the day you brought her in here, Sally…but…"

"No ifs, ands, or buts, Louie. I'm embarrassed and I apologize," Sally seethed.

Sally Glasses took out a wad of cash from his front pant pocket and peeled off three tens which he squeezed into grandpa's hand, adding a kiss to his cheek.

Thirty dollars. My grandparents' rent was twenty-four dollars a month in those days.

Louie Brown, Uncle Bill, and Connie, the bartender, walked to the front window of the Half Moon in time to catch Sally Glasses "smacking the piss" out of blondie.

The next night, Sally came into the restaurant with his wife, sat at a different table, of course, had a very nice meal complete with an after-dinner pizza and two Tortoni desserts.

The following Friday night, at precisely seven-thirty, there was Sally Glasses at his usual table, with his Rob-Roy waiting. The jukebox was playing Rosemary Clooney's *Come on-a My House.*

The redhead Sally brought that night was even more stunning than the blonde.

THE KID WHO STOLE THE CAN OPENER

I'm really not sure what his name was. I think they called him Ronnie, but to us he would always be known as: THE KID WHO STOLE THE CAN OPENER.

It was 1957 in the Belmont section of the Bronx. Dion and the Belmonts were still harmonizing on the street corners in the neighborhood. Mickey Mantle was on his way to winning the Triple Crown of baseball. Chevrolet came out with arguably the best car they ever produced, President Eisenhower kept us in peace, established NASA, and played a lot of golf. And most importantly, the Puerto Ricans had not yet taken over the Bronx.

Life was good…better than good.

Maureen Roach had already been through the fifth grade when her brother John and I had just finished our first year with the Dominican Sisters. Maureen had already been mean spirited, and the nuns had completed her malicious character by the time she was eleven.

When Maureen baby sat us, she walked around with a twelve -inch ruler and a dish towel over her head, smacking us for any infraction that she deemed suitable for corporal punishment. She swung the ruler often. Maureen also pinched and pulled hair. She was destined to become a Mother Superior in the Dominican Sisters order. Or perhaps an S & M mistress.

This one torrid, July day, Maureen took us to the playground that ran from Crotona Avenue to East 182nd Street. In those days, it was perfectly fine and safe for Maureen and her two friends, also in being mean training with the nuns, to take two six year olds on the five-block walk to the playground. In those days, in that area, everything was protected by some tough guys.

The park was boarded by two bocce courts on the Crotona side andon the other side, St. Martin of Tours Church and Aquinas Hall High School. Aquinas also had a convent which housed the good sisters.

Maureen would make it a point every so often to make us look up at the gold cross atop St. Martins and bless ourselves and say a Hail Mary. When we got to the part, "*...and thy womb, Jesus,*" if we didn't bow our heads…whack with the ruler, usually on our hands or the back of the leg, the thigh actually, because it hurt more there.

If a nun passed the playground carrying a bag of groceries back to the convent, Maureen would point and say, "John, Louis…hurry," and it became a race to see who would get there first and tote the brown bag for the sister.

Being that the playground was under the windows of Aquinas Hall, and in full view of the Mother Superior's room, we were to always be on our best behavior, and Maureen made sure of that. Her friends were her backup in case her back was momentarily turned.

We arrived at the park with a basket for a nice picnic. Peanut butter and jelly sandwiches on white Wonder bread. A big bag of Wise potato chips, and a few ten cent bottles of Pepsi Cola. The Irish kids always drank Pepsi, the Italian kids, only Coke. The Irish also used Jif peanut butter, but we knew better with Skippy. These were among the serious differences that we all learned to tolerate somehow.

Also in the basket were a few napkins, Maureen's ruler, a black St, Joseph's Missal, and a red and yellow Baltimore Catechism. Maureen and her friends asked us questions. John knew all the answers and I shook my head.

Oh, and the basket also carried a can opener for the Pepsi Colas. The silver-colored job with a pointed can opener on one end and a rounded bottle opener on the other.

The playground was much like any other urban, outdoor play area. All asphalt, no grass, a small tree here or there that was planted in a cut out in the macadam, and smelled of dog urine. We had a sliding pond as we called it, but most normal folks would call it just a slide. There were twelve-foot monkey bars, three swings, one for toddlers, and a see-saw. And of course, the ubiquitous sandbox. Every park in the city of New York had to have one so dogs could…

John and I were digging around in the sandbox, being careful of the lumps of course, with our army men. We only had ten men each. That made a squad. This day I was the Germans.

Suddenly Maureen and her two friends came running to the sandbox in sheer terror.

"John, Louis…that kid over there stole our can opener," Maureen screamed. She pointed in the direction of the Park House, a small almost hut like building that housed the rest rooms, the 'Parkey's room, and the water fountain. John and I looked at each other in total shock and abandoned our war in the desert to investigate the robbery. Mind you we are both six at this time. I guess Maureen and the other 'nuns-in-training' just needed a male figure to sacrifice.

There he was! He stood well over six feet tall. His brown eyes bulged out of his head, resembling a frog-like creature. His neck was way too long for his body, and his Adam's apple protruded in a most peculiar way. It looked as if the boy had swallowed a golf ball or a lemon. The protruding, bucked teeth finished the look telling us he was just not right.

John and I made our way over to the park house as if we were sneaking up on something dangerous, all the while Maureen encouraging us to attack like the Crusaders did for Christ. Mama didn't raise no fool, Sister Maureen. These things take planning.

As we approached the kid, he was noisily slurping from the water fountain, his oversized lips directly on the spout as if he was sucking the water out of it.

"Excuse me? Do you have our can opener?" I dared say. My knees were shaking by now.

Suddenly and without warning, the kid who stole the can opener reeled around from the fountain. Water was all over his white t-shirt and dripping down from his chin like the Creature From the Black Lagoon. He made a horrible guttural noise that sounded like, "Fuck you," or maybe it was, "Yes, I do." John and I discussed this moment for years to attempt a translation.

The kid who stole the can opener walked away from us, giving a momentary smile at the three girls who ran screaming to the safety of the blanket and the picnic basket with the holy books.

It was more of a lanky gait than a walk. The kid-who-stole-the-can-opener's arms were weirdly straight down by his sides, not moving front to back, and they seemed way too long. His feet were gargantuan and instead of U.S. Keds or Converse sneakers he wore these black shoes with the laces on the side that old Jewish people had worn back then.

We were terrified, but determined to get back our can opener or get our revenge.

Maureen called for a meeting back at the blanket. John and I gathered up our army men as we now had a bigger battle to pursue.

Maureen began the meeting with a prayer invoking Jesus, Mary, and Joseph, and about six saints. I forgot to bow my head at the name of Jesus and out came the ruler from the picnic basket and whack, on the knuckles.

By now, the kid who stole the can opener was at the bocce courts watching the old geeps play a serious money game. A geep is an Italian laborer who uses his pick and shovel all day at a comfortable pace. He stops for fifteen minutes for some bread and salami and a bit of wine before he gets back to work.

The bocce court was a level below the playground, separated by a sixteen-foot silver colored, chain link fence.

I don't recall now if it was my idea or John's, but it was decided to fill up a family size bottle of Coca-Cola, that we found in the trash basket, with fountain water. We were going to spill the water on the kid who stole the can opener.

We took our plan to the triumvirate of Maureen and her two friends. The premenstrual trio decided that we could do what we needed to do.

Maureen said, "Do with him what you will," mimicking Pontius Pilate's hand washing scene.

John and I filled the Coke bottle slowly as we were careful not to touch where the kid who stole the can opener's lips had touched. John gagged a few times as the bottle filled with the cold water.

Off we went with the Coke bottle to the spot in the playground above the bocce courts.

John and I looked through the chain link fence, until we spied the kid who stole the can opener, sitting among the Italian geeps. The old men were shouting out instructions, in Italian to their partners and friends. "Shoot the palino." "Get close to the first green ball, Vito." "I lost twenty-five cents on you, Antonio, vaffanculo," and other words of encouragement.

Carefully, we picked one of the chain link squares to be the spot we would use to put the opening of the Coke bottle, spilling the water on the head of the unsuspecting kid who stole the can opener.

"Bombs away!' John said. We both held the bottle as the water chugged out. Immediately screams from below were heard in Italian and broken English. John was the smartest kid I knew in school but he knew nothing about wind trajectory and leading the target from our first year with Sister Jarleth.

One voice was heard above all. My Sicilian born grandfather, Gaspare Miceli, was one of the bocce men who got soaked from above. Luckily for me, Grandpa didn't recognize me and my Irish thug friend, John.

The last thing I saw before we took flight to the safety of the picnic blanket, was the kid who stole the can opener looking up at us, covering his funny looking mouth and with both hands, jumping up and down in total hysteria.

He was bone dry.

After a while, John and I were back in the sandbox with our army men. Later, we all went back to the Roach family apartment where Maureen started a rosary.

Thirty years later I was walking on East 187th Street on my way to a business lunch and there he was; the kid who stole the can opener.

His disability was now more evident to me. He looked very much the same except he now had gray hair on his temples. I paused to remember the day we came across him in the playground in 1957, never retrieving Maureen's can opener. His white haired elderly mother led the way as they walked with their shopping bags. What would become of him when she was gone? Poor guy.

By the way. Maureen never became a nun. She married a cop, had as few kids and got divorced. I think her cop husband couldn't deal with the ruler.

REPORT CARD DAY

Every six weeks report card day came up in Sister Mary's seventh grade class.

It was nineteen sixty-two and I was 12 years old.

There wasn't a thing called obsessive-compulsive disorder back in those days, but Sister Mary surely had it.

Our class of thirty-seven pupils, consisted of the boys, all in white shirts, navy blue pants, blue school ties with the school insignia, and black, lace up shoes, and the girls, in those gorgeous, pleated blue and white skirts and white blouses, buttoned all the way to the neck. The skirts were below the knee and finished with penny loafers and white ankle socks.

Good Sister Mary, a woman in her mid-thirties, wore the habit of the Sisters of Charity. A long black gown, a large set of rosary beads looped around her waist with the crucifix hanging six inches below her midsection. Her unknown color of hair was pulled back into her black bonnet that covered her forehead and both sides of her face. She wore a gold wedding band, third finger, left hand, as she was married to Jesus.

Everything was perfect and uniform except the seating arrangements.

Sister Mary had six rows of student desks, six pupils per row plus one extra as the last seat in the sixth row. That last seat drove her crazy, I'm sure.

Sister had it in her mind that the students should be seated in order of their grades, each row designated by our alphabetic achievement.

Row A was where the really smart kids sat. Three Irish girls, two Irish boys, and one Puerto Rican named Edmund.

Row B? Two rows, with a mix of Italian kids whose parents were 'prominent,' aka 'donated a lot of money,' to the parish: The local undertaker's son, the daughter of the Italian restaurant owner where the priests would eat free, the police captain in the 43rd precinct's daughter, and three, Con Ed managers' kids.

Row C, my row, was comprised of six pupils of no merit whatsoever, so they told us. Never to move from steerage to first class unless someone in the B row got polio or hepatitis B. I was locked in the fourth seat in the C row. It was Devil's Island, from which there was no escape.

Row D, E, and F were interchangeable losers who were presumed to be future death row inmates. They were a mix of fat, polish kids, Puerto Ricans who barely understood English, and blacks who were marking time, awaiting expulsion at any moment. Perhaps some of those kids did become death row inmates, but if they did, I would guess it would be more for the way they were treated in my school than where they came from. After all, I sure felt the sting, and I was in a row 'ahead' of them

There was a buildup of either excitement or terror, depending upon your row classification when report card day was approaching. All test papers and pop quiz grades were added up, divided by the number of tests and quizzes, flipped and flopped, with I'm sure being Irish got you extra credit, and put into one, big, bold letter form on the front of the rectangular, gray card, and, to make matters worse, the six subjective categories such as obedience, completes tasks on time, and works well with others, was on the flip side.

For me, the Sunday night before report card day was nothing but tossing and turning because I knew what was coming. My stomach would be in knots, and I would break into a cold sweat in my bed and I was sure my mother would think the next day that I'd wet the bed or something. But, rather than study harder in a futile attempt to move away from Sing-Sing prison and into the B Row, I did what any kid would do when, in what was felt an impossible situation to get out of, I would play with my baseball card collection and watch Bonanza.

The morning of the fateful day was a combination of my churning stomach and a tight sphincter muscle. No food, no water; nothing could stay down. I'm sure the moms of the A row kids, those mother fuckers, made bacon and eggs with toast and orange juice like in Lassie or Leave it to Beaver. At any rate, my stomach was doing flips and ignoring hunger, now causing my head to also ache.

Lining up to enter class was like getting ready to be summarily executed. Monsignor Blake, a cross between Basil Rathbone and Broderick Crawford was to soon be handing out the report cards.

Monsignor was scheduled to be in our classroom at 10:30 that morning. Sister Mary barked out our orders like the Commandant of Stalag 17.

Desks had to be wiped clean, our books inside the desk had to be in perfect size order with no papers askew, a nearly impossible task. Pencils had to be sharpened and placed neatly in the little tray next to the books. Two boys, usually the taller ones, took a big, yellowish, damp sponge and wiped the blackboard clean of any marks or chalk powder. They were tasked with wiping in vertical lines so absolutely no swirls were evident.

We watched the clock as it approached the arrival of Monsignor. I kept my butt as tight as a crab's ass so emissions of stomach gas had no chance to escape.

Sister Mary stood at attention, near the classroom door, the report cards wrapped neatly by a rubber band and held in her sweaty hands.

The moment arrived as Monsignor filled the door like Count Dracula in his flowing black cape. I nearly shit myself seeing the huge man who looked like he ate babies for breakfast enter the room. I trembled and my eyes were as large as saucers and fixated on this intimidating 'man of God'. He wore a regal, black, four cornered hat with a red pom-pon on top.

Sister had a plastic frog clicker and when she squeezed it, it made a noise like the sound of my grandfather's knees. That perilous sound seemed to echo loudly and boom in my ears. With that sound, as one, we stood from our desks to attention. I don't know if we were told it or not, but I was so scared that my eyes never diverted from the man in the front of our classroom, so I have no idea if my friends were as scared as I.

Monsignor took his hands out from under his cape, calmly took the report cards from Sister Mary, who looked up at him adoringly, smiling like she just hit the Irish Sweepstakes. He bowed his head toward the door signaling the nun to close it. The moment of reckoning was upon us.

The nun stood to the side as Monsignor stepped onto the riser in front of the class where her desk was. He looked like a giant behemoth which now I know was all part of their plan to minimize us, make us feel inferior.

Our hands were clasped together and held upon our desktops, a position we had actually practiced under the watchful eye of Sister Mary. We awaited our fates.

Monsignor Dracula slowly and dramatically removed the rubber band from the report cards. He cleared his throat, a sound I've only since heard in the men's room of shot and beer saloons. He always seemed to have a lot of built up phlegm to clear.

He got to the task at hand.

"Kathleen O'Rourke!" he announced.

The girl in the first row, first seat stood and walked up to Monsignor, looking up at him like he was God Almighty. Sister Mary was jittery, biting her lower lip, her eyes opened twice their normal size.

Monsignor continued. He read her grades aloud.

"A, A, A, A, A, A, A." He smiled down knowingly at the red-headed, freckled face before him. He then flipped the card over in a flourish.

"A, A, A, A, A, A, A…Very nice work, Kathleen…How is your grandmother doing?"

"Thank you, Monsignor. She is home in Ireland visiting our family," Kathleen answered in her angelic, sweet voice. I wanted to puke.

Dracula smiled and I would have sworn I saw fangs. Sister Mary lightly bit her index finger and moved uncomfortably from one foot to the other.

"John Joseph Donahue," Monsignor announced.

A streak of blond hair flashed front and center.

"A, A, A, A, A, A, A." Similar grades were read from the back of the report card. "Very nice job, my boy. Please tell your saint of a mother that I'll be at supper tomorrow night. Tell her not to fuss too much," Monsignor blurted. Sister cleared her throat and looked down momentarily at the floor. I could tell, but did not understand at the time why she was uncomfortable with that comment.

"Thank you, Monsignor. Yes, I will tell her, Monsignor," John Joseph replied.

Soon I would be standing in front of the cloaked giant.

This went on through the A row students. When he got to Edmund Diaz, and he announced the kid's name, he glanced quickly at the nun. His facial expression was a tell. Without words, he was saying, *How could a Puerto Rican be so smart?*

Monsignor read Edmund's grades quickly and nearly fell off the riser handing the kid his report card. No pleasantries were exchanged like he did to the immediate pupil before Edmund, telling the girl, Mary Alice McGinnity, that he would be by later that day to bless the new baby's crib.

I looked over at Sister Mary. She was moving quickly from foot to foot in those hideous, black nun shoes. I swore I saw a small puddle of water under her feet.

The B row was uneventful. One kid was told he could do better in Math, another was told to apply herself, and one was told to say a Novena in the hope that the Blessed Mother would help his grades.

Sister's handkerchief was now fully in her mouth. Her blue eyes looked as if they were rolling back in her head. I was afraid she would pass out. The puddle seemed bigger. My eyes darted back and forth between her puddle, her face, and the monsignor. My heart was racing and pounding so hard I was sure Mary Ellen McGrath next to me in row B could hear it.

The girl in the first seat in the C Row, just a few seats ahead of me had her grades read by Monsignor.

C, B, B minus, C, C, B…the flip side was better but still mostly B's.

Monsignor glared at her from his perch until the poor girl cried. Sister Mary was in her own world and let out a low moan that she tried to cover with a cough.

The boy behind the first girl in my row fared a bit worse. His arrival at the front of the classroom, his penance for being a C student, was the Monsignor literally pulling his already tussled, brown hair, the poor kid making a face of excruciation. Between the physical pain and his embarrassment, I'm sure he was united with the crucified Jesus, but there would probably never be any glorious resurrection for this young man. My stress increased and I felt my ass pucker; suddenly, I emitted a flash of odious gas. My face turned as red as a beet.

The next kid up front got more of the same treatment. His hair was pulled and his ear lobe was twisted. He tried hard not to cry. When my glance returned to Sister, she had her hands folded low in front of her, which I thought was odd, and was nervously fingering the beads from her rosary that fell below her waist and rapidly tapping the end of the crucifix against her holy gown. I swear even today, I saw a few drops of what I then thought to be sweat, splash from under her habit onto the puddle beneath her.

It was now my turn!

You would think a man who spoke Latin could pronounce an Italian name. "Louis Ra-MAN-o," he said, butchering my name which I swear was intentional.

I cautiously walked to the front of the room.

He read my grades aloud, but due to my trepidation and fear, I didn't even hear him. I just stood, head down, and waited for the hair pulling or ear twisting to begin. My legs were like putty.

"Look at me! These grades are simply awful," Monsignor bellowed. Simultaneously as he spoke and I looked up at him, his four fingers slammed across my face snapping my head like a prize fighter getting a left hook. I never saw it coming. My ears rang and I nearly puked on his shoes. I think I smelled whisky when the Monsignor exhaled from his exertion.

The nun's gaspy moan I thought was her abhorrence to the situation which I was sure she would be reprimanded herself for, but years later, I would understand that she was really headed toward an orgasm!

I staggered back to my desk, my face red from being struck by the beefy, freckled hand making solid contact with it and of course from the embarrassment, while Sister staggered a bit herself and just kept repeating lowly, "Oh, my God, oh, my God."'

Sister Mary offered a glass of ice water to the Monsignor. She was panting heavily, and she momentarily slipped on her wet spot but was graceful nonetheless as she walked from the fountain out in the hall back into our classroom.

He smiled and gave a knowing glance toward Sister, and drank it down in three gulps before he continued his carnage.

By the time Monsignor was through with the D, E, and F rows, half the class had the shit kicked out of them. Sister's moan-coughs were coming at a more rapid pace and were getting more high pitched. Her face was turning red and a few wet hairs began peeking through her bonnet.

The last of the F row, a wild-eyed, black girl named Angela, who was my friend, bopped up to get her report card, defiant in the face of a potential beating.

Something about her demeanor gave pause to the maniacal arm flailing of the now nearly exhausted cleric. He growled at Angela and flung the report card at her.

With a catlike move Angela snagged the card in mid-air and in one move turned on her heels and walked back to her desk.

Sister Mary looked as if she needed a cigarette or something.

As Monsignor started to leave the room, on cue, Kathleen O'Rourke, whose address in our classroom was, and always would be, first row, first seat, stood.

"Monsignor, may we have your blessing?"

"Why of course, Kathleen," Monsignor answered.

Sister Mary reached for her frog clicker and again slipped in the puddle she had made. Click-click…we all stood…click-click…we all knelt.

Holding the drape of his cape out of the way with his left hand, and with a theatrical flourish, Monsignor made the sign of the cross in our direction with his right hand and bellowed, "In nomine Patris, et Filii, et Spiritus Sancti, Amen."

The frog made another click and we returned to our seats. Sister Mary was a wet mess of enjoyment.

She lovingly paused at the door as the pom-pon topped cleric exited the room, all smiles and sweetness. All smiles and sweetness, that is, until her head spun around like Regan MacNeil in the movie The Exorcist. The door snapped shut.

The good Sister looked in the direction of the C, D, E, and F rows and pronounced in her shrill voice, "You've embarrassed me for the last time!"

I let loose with the biggest fart of my life.

EGGS

In some ways, we were guerilla warriors. Well, at least we thought we were, but we were not very good in battle. Bullshit and brains were our weapons and shields. Running was our fallback position.

Six of us, Joe, Rocky, Joey, Eddie, Johnny and Louie, that's me, were a group of Catholic school sixteen-year-olds, living in a Bronx housing project that, like a fine wine when beyond its peak, had already started to turn.

"An idle mind is the devil's workshop," the nuns said and they were spot on this particular crisp November evening in 1966. We were bored to tears in the aftermath of Halloween, when the mayhem of putting colored ground chalk and white flour into long athletic socks, tying them off and smacking the piss out of people and property. The day after Halloween it was over and no one would show up with those silly socks until next year.

Dr. Martin Luther King Jr. was fighting for civil rights for the, "so called negro" as Malcolm X had called people of color. They were two men fighting for equality albeit down two totally separate paths. King preached non-violence, Malcolm wanted equality "by any means necessary." I liked them both.

The blacks were more confused than we were, so they picked a side whenever a particular situation called for peace or fighting. It was like a menu. Brother Malcolm said, "Fuck whitey, they want to keep us in chains." Dr. King said, "Love is the only force capable of transferring and enemy into a friend."

Both philosophies would be tested this particular night.

"Let's go get some eggs and see what happens," I said.

"Whose got money for that shit? I can put two gallons of gas in my car for the price of a dozen eggs. Fuck that," Joe said. He was older than the rest of us by a year and was thinking car before he even had one.

"What are you, hanging out with Sol and Jerry Wasserman again? A buck twenty and we have two dozen eggs. Four each, two in each of our jacket pockets and we are ready for battle," Rocky said. He was always the most pragmatic and broke things down analytically to where they made sense. All he needed was a book of matches, an incendiary device like me, to light the fuse.

Everyone agreed and off we went to Good Food, a small, Jewish run grocery slash deli on Lafayette and Soundview Avenue. The store owners were holding on for dear life as the neighborhood was going down like the whores in Hunts Point. Soon, they would not be able to keep up with the customers stealing everything in sight. A little fire, some insurance money, and off to Florida Jack and his brother Lew would go. End of an era.

Our group of six all wore black leather jackets. Not the Marlon Brando in The Wild One kind of jacket but a dress jacket which looked more like a coat. A pocket for each hand, two eggs in every pocket.

It was cold enough when the wind whipped around the buildings to make my nose run. The eggs were kept warm by the fabric inside the pocket of the jackets. I had both hands on the eggs, handling them like a gunslinger paws his six-shooters. I noticed that all the others were doing the same.

It was dark, about eight thirty at night with a half-moon lit, star peppered sky. All six of us were looking for a target for an egg pelting. A bus, a parked truck, the protestant church, the police room on the ground level of Joes building? We needed something more noble, more memorable, more important than mundane targets like the A & P or the American Gas Station.

It seemed that Rocky and I spotted the target at the same split second.

About fifty, maybe sixty yards away, beyond two, six-foot high chain link fences, under a lamp post with a dull bulb, in front of the one level community center building was the object of our egg pummeling.

A group of black guys, looked like about ten of them, had huddled together smoking some weed and talking about who knows what? Every one of the young men wore a hat of some kind. Wool skull caps pulled over their foreheads, Yankee hats, one or two African style skull caps, most dressed in high school varsity jackets or leather coats like ours.

"Rocco, can we reach?" The Roman candle was lit.

"I see no problem. Maybe Joey can't cause he has no arm but he will come close enough and the splash will mess up their cons," Rocco said referring to their Chuck Taylor Converse All-Star sneakers. The black guys wore white high tops. We wore the black low tops. Go figure.

The order went out. "We rapid fire the eggs at the yamms." Melanzane is the word for eggplant in Italian. In dialect it became malanga... the derivative became yamm. There were sixty other pejoratives but yamm and spear-chuckers were most widely used and accepted.

The darkness and the cover of some twelve food trees along with the poor outdoor lighting gave us the natural advantage. The target could not see us clear enough to see our faces. All they would see is that it was white guys. That isn't enough for retaliation in the light of day.

The eggs flew in rapid succession, two dozen fresh eggs many hitting their marks splat against the side of a face here, a beanie top there, a shoulder, a neck, sneakers. We fled in stealth silence hearing our mothers called all kinds of horrible things. The six of us split up instinctively into pairs with instructions to meet up in thirty minutes, blocks away from the target area at Rosario's Pizzeria.

The troops reconnoitered as planned each ordering our own slice and coke. Joe was thinking how much gas he could put into his car, but the aroma from the oven was too much for him to resist.

We talked in hushed tones so no one could hear that we were the culprits of the most-dastardly sneak attack since Pearl Harbor.

"It's quarter to ten. My parents think I went to study at the school library. I gotta go," Eddie said. Eddie was a masterful storyteller who could convince a cloistered nun to remove her panties.

"Me, too. My folks think I'm helping blind kids after guitar practice. See ya tomorrow night," Johnny said.

We all split up in twos to go to our separate buildings into the warmth of our beds and Playboy books. No way would we travel in a group after the ruthless attack on the so-called negroes.

Joe and I walked toward my building, hands inside our leather coats to keep warm from the colder late evening air. Joe's building was not far from mine and he would be fine going the rest of the way home alone.

As we approached my building a sea of black enveloped Joe and me cornering us against one of those six-foot chain link fences. Six guys in front of us and six guys at our backs behind the fence. We had nowhere to run, climb, hide, simply no escape. Fighting would be a joke against such odds. I figured, we catch a good ass kicking, cover up to save our heads and faces and be done with it.

"You the motherfuckers that threw eggs at us?" An angry Sonny Liston look-alike demanded.

Joe wasn't much of a talker so it was all me.

"Eggs? Someone was crazy enough to throw eggs at you guys? When? Here? Tonight?" I questioned.

"Yeah, you midget fuck. Right here. Look at my jacket?" Another victim blurted. The yellow yoke had properly stained his purple cloth school basketball jacket.

"Man, that is fucked up, "I added.

"I think you were in with those guys and we are about to fuck you up," Liston said.

"I swear to God we just got off the bus, had some pizza and we were going home. We weren't even around here tonight," I pled.

Joe just waited and watched the magic.

Suddenly, a familiar voice came from behind the chain links.

"Louie, you sure it wasn't you?" Freddy Gallo said.

Freddy had long ago gone to the dark side. We were in the same class from fifth through eighth-grade and were friendly. We even played ball together although he was a phenomenal athlete. Freddy was just like a so-called negro. He walked like them, wore their kind of sneakers, talked like them, wore weighted ankle bracelets to help him jump higher on the basketball court, and went out with colored girls.

"Hey Freddy! What's up? Nah, we were at my school playing some hoops and just got back here. Like half an hour ago. We're both late now."

Freddy looked me dead in the eyes from between the chain links.

"Louie…let me smell your fingers," Freddy commanded.

My hands, all of the marauders hands for that matter reeked from the Sulphur of the warming eggs in our jacket pockets. It's not the kind of aroma that wears off. I got a good whiff of the acrid smell when I was eating my slice of pizza.

Slowly I raised both of my hands up to Freddy's nose.

He kept looking in my eyes. He took a big whiff of my fingers through the fence and his eyes blinked from the stench.

I lowered my hands back into my pockets never taking my eyes off his.

"Nah, it's not them ...they cool," Freddy announced.

"See you guys," I said.

"Take care," Joe trembled.

Liston turned around and got into my space.

"Yo, Louie, lemme hold a quarter."

I gave him fifty cents.

THE DAY KENNEDY DIED

-A YOUNG BOY'S PERSPECTIVE

The weather was beautiful this late November day in the Bronx. No coats were needed, and the crew of thirteen-year-old boys were looking forward to playing touch football back in the neighborhood after school. Sweatshirts or sweaters would be all that would be needed this particular day for the three on three, best of five, twenty-one-point matchup that would likely be called due to darkness that evening. We generally played until no one could see the ball, lost in the shadows of the fourteen and eight-story housing project buildings. The occasional street lamps were too dingy or too dead to illuminate the asphalt playground that we called our home field.

The school lunch was cruel. Not because the food was bad. It was quite good at times. Today it was rice topped with an oniony chicken chow mein, with more celery than chicken, but tasty. String beans, a container of semi-cold, whole milk, and a peach half in a sugary syrup that made my cavities hurt enough to pucker my cheeks. The combination of foods gave the class enough gas to power a locomotive.

I sat next to this red-headed Irish kid who hated everything that had ever been served to him except the milk and margarine-soaked white bread. I quietly, without bringing the trade to the attention of the trained Nazi in a black habit, passed my bread under the table. A quick scoop landed the faux Chinese meal into my green plastic plate, and I dug into the meal like I was starving.

The meal was cruel because we are not allowed to speak while we ate lunch. Not before, during, or after the meal could we utter a sound or do anything but facial expressions to let each other know what we were thinking. The Irish kid sat across from me on a long, metal table that sat eight boys on either side, girls separated from the boys naturally, so hormones could not collide. The Irish kid pointed to his plate, then to his pink, outstretched tongue with the international sign for vomit. I pointed to the sliced, white bread with the Oleo margarine, and the deal was consummated quickly.

Just imagine being a new teenager and being subjected to eating your lunch in silence, surrounded by your friends and classmates, and then folding your hands in prayerful contemplation. Simply cruel.

Entering the overheated classroom after such a hearty lunch, I could feel my eyes drooping with my already diminished attention span. The only thing that kept me from falling onto the chair-desk's surface directly on my face was the blue and white, Catholic school girl, pleated skirts of Joyce LaRusso and Loida Milan.

Sister Nazi of the Face of Jesus commanded us to take out our math books. My stomach flipped because Algebra was another forced cruelty. I could taste the chow mein onions in my throat, and my lower intestine grumbled in agreement.

Suddenly, the tapping of the school's intercom brought everyone's attention to the speaker, which hung to the right of the crucified Jesus. Everyone looked at the box on the wall as if it were alive, waiting for the commandant's voice to speak the next cruel set of rules. Someone called the nuns snakes with tits.

This time, the tapping seemed to go on a few more hits than usual.

"Attention please…attention, please…Boys and girls, sisters and lay teachers. Please pray for President Kennedy. There has been an accident."

That was it. No information. Just an accident.

I pictured a car accident on the Bruckner Expressway in the Bronx where numerous accidents led to people punching each other or were dragged away in an ambulance, bloodied or covered. I shrugged my shoulders but was happy that there was at least a temporary reprieve from the Algebra lesson. My stomach eased a bit.

The nun waddled over to a bookcase behind her desk, almost tripping on the six-inch riser that made her desk seem like it towered over the daily inmates. She snapped on the brown box radio that sat atop the bookcase and waited until the tubes inside the antique "warmed-up."

"...several shots hit President Kennedy. His motorcade, including Vice President Johnson, rushed off to nearby Parkland Hospital. The president is said to be in grave condition..."

"Let's all pray students, please get out of your seats and onto your knees and all ask for Our Lady to intercede for the president and his family," the nun said through a stream of tears. The girls were holding their hands to their mouths or sobbed into their tissues draped in black rosary beads.

"The President of the United States is dead," the radio reporter announced. The gasps in the classroom turned into sobs. No boys cried.

A few minutes later, the intercom tapped again, this time only three taps. They did a lot of things in threes over here. The whole trinity-superstition-repetition thing.

"Attention please...attention please...we are having an immediate dismissal in five minutes. The entire student body will go to the church to say a prayer for the repose of the soul of our beloved President Kennedy. School will be closed tomorrow."

I thought I had died and gone to heaven. No algebra, at least for the moment, almost two hours off today, and off all day tomorrow, and it wasn't a holy day of obligation. Maybe there really is a God!

After a three-second prayer at the church with the priest all dressed up in his gown, flailing incense at the altar, the guys with heads lowered in humility for the sake of the sisters, and knowing that they would pay dearly for any infraction on the next school day, left the church, moving quickly toward the neighborhood.

"I bet they used a powerful rifle...like an elephant gun," one kid blurted.

"My father's gonna be happy. He says that Kennedy is nothing but an Irish fuck," another reported.

"Johnson did it. He hates the Kennedys. You can see it in his hillbilly face," I announced.

"Nah, the Russians all the way. We are going to war over this… fucking guaranteed," the elephant gun expert said.

Back at the projects where we all lived, we scattered like cockroaches to our home buildings, hearing the instructions from one of the guys as we bolted. "Choose up in fifteen at one hundred. You slow, you blow." In English...we would select teams in fifteen minutes at P.S. 100 school yard. If you came late you were omitted from play.

Three Jewish men, two with numbers tattooed on their arms, spoke in a blend of English and Yiddish. They seemed more unsettled and worried about the assassination than the three moms who rocked and short rolled their strollers to keep their babies quiet. The women were mentioning Jackie and the two kids.

The mailman arrived and made his way to the bank of one hundred and twenty-six stainless steel mailboxes in the lobby. Some called it a vestibule to make it sound fancy.

The three Jews followed quickly behind the letter carrier, hoping that he had some information other than everyone heard from the radio watching Walter Cronkite choke up. After all, the mailman was a federal employee, he should know.

I scurried into the elevator and pressed nine. A black lady, she was called a negro at the time, got into the cab and pressed eleven. She hung her head low murmuring to herself.

"This is bad. This is really bad."

My Grandma Rose was standing at the ironing board, pressing anything that was in the yellow, plastic clothes basket at her feet.

"Louis, the president was shot. He's dead! Oh, Dio!" she cried, invoking God.

"I know grandma, I'm going to play football. Be back at five thirty. What's for supper?"

"God willing, pasta passili and a frittata ensalada. Maybe you should stay home today, Louis." Peas and macaroni and an omelette.

"Can't do it. Three-day tournament. I'm quarterback. Gotta go."

My school clothes and shoes flew off into a pile, replaced by a pair of black chinos, a sweatshirt, and Chuck Taylor Converse All-Star sneakers, low back, with black socks.

"He should die and go right to hell and rot there."

"Who, grandma?"

"The man who shot the president. They should torture him, rip his eyes out, and then hang him."

"Oh, yeah. They should!" I agreed while I looked for the football.

"Poor Jackie and the babies. Madonna, Mia. I hope he burns in hell forever. I put the horns on him," Grandma cried.

She cried for days.

What seemed like an eternity later, it was only a day or two, still at the ironing board, Grandma Rose cursed the shooter as he was brought out by the Texas police. Oswald was his name. Lee Harvey Oswald. Assassins always have three names for some reason.

"He should get struck by a bolt of lightning, that murderer."

At that very moment, a man in a suit and fedora hat reached in and threw a shot into Oswald. The crowd of cops seemed to fall into a heap, struggling with the shooter.

Grandma Rose, her eyes as big a demi-tasse cups gasped at the black and white scene.

"O, Dio," she muttered. At that moment, she stopped crying and continued ironing my white polyester school shirt.

She was convinced that the malocchio, the evil eye she put on Oswald, worked. She never mentioned it again.

That afternoon, my team won the tournament. I tossed a bomb to Fat Joe who made a spectacular over-the-shoulder catch in the end zone, leaving his defender crumbled on the black macadam.

On Monday morning, first thing after prayers for Kennedy and President Johnson, reality hit hard.

"Please take out your Algebra books."

I tasted bile in my throat for the first time in days.

KARMA

DeKalb Avenue and 212th Street in the North Bronx was a typical urban neighborhood back in 1969. Cookie cutter apartment buildings lined the streets with each boulevard adorning the same maple trees as the next.

First and second generation working class people made up the vicinity, their children all striving to get into colleges in an effort to escape the humdrum life they led. Some were looking to avoid the draft and the Vietnam War, some looking to learn how to live through education, and some simply trying for a good, secure job working for the city.

Allan Fischer, 19 years old, and his friends were not overly concerned about the draft as they were the few who were enrolled in local colleges and obtained a 2-S student deferment because of it. Allan was especially not concerned as his draft number was three hundred eleven out of a possible three hundred sixty-five, and the military was only up to number ninety-five. He was a lock not to get his greetings from Uncle Sam. This was their final summer of childhood and they were going to make the best of it.

On one particularly torrid Sunday afternoon in July, when fire hydrants were opened to cool down the kids, and fresh cut watermelon and lemon ice were passed around to refresh everyone who sat on the stoops of the five and six story pre-World War II elevator buildings, Allan and his friends got to work on their too-much-time-on-their-hands mischief.

The scruffy bunch, with long hair, as made popular by the infamous Beatles, sat on the stoop at 2350 DeKalb Avenue in their shorts, and white, Converse All-Star sneakers. Together, they watched the afternoon parade of sweaty people pass by. Girls in their pedal pushers with somewhat see-through blouses going to the store for their mothers were the group's favorite scenery, but invariably, someone in Allan's group would make a snide remark about some of the less fortunate in their neighborhood who were walking past their building.

"Oh, shit! Here he comes, Farquad. Look at him! The simple bastard looks like he was rode hard and put up wet," Bruce Rosen, Allan's closest childhood friend announced. Bruce, a tad shorter than the diminutive Allan, also had long, scraggly, brown hair tied in the back with rubber bands, made into a make-shift ponytail and was one of the more outspoken of the group.

"What a retard! There's just something not right about him. He's a few cards short of a full deck," Allan added, shaking his head. Everyone laughed. Allan always thought he had real cool quips and that the other guys could only wish they had his repertoire of come-backs.

"Look at this mope. His mother must be so proud," Lenny Burns, another one of the gang of five, added.

The poor target in question was a sixty-year old, dim-witted man who lived his entire life in a one-bedroom apartment across the street with his now aged mother. His real name was Samuel Wasserman, but the group nicknamed him Farquad, and Sammy the Retard. Poor Sammy was frightened by the group of five teens and would often guffaw when they ranted and cursed at him, as if he were approving their meanness, even though it really hurt him inside. He always bravely held back the tears until he got past them.

"Sammy, you retard! Get your fat ass over here and tie my sneakers," Bruce bellowed.

Sammy, insanely obese and almost as pale as an Albino, towered over six feet tall. The young men should have been afraid of him, but they knew he was feeble-minded and taunted him every chance they got. "Nice hat!" one would shout as he sported a worn, New York Mets hat, over a mop of hair that was butchered monthly by his mother. During the summer, Sammy always wore a white, V-neck t-shirt with the stains of his last two meals adorning the front of it. His cheap sneakers, what were called skips back in those days, were originally white, but so stained and worn they became rust colored. Sammy wore horn-rimmed glasses with a knot of adhesive tape attaching one of the arms to the frames. "Hey, four-eyes!" would be yelled at him as he ambled by. He walked with the gait of a disturbed person with his mouth open and his dark-circled eyes always flashing mostly toward the sky. His belly had three layers of fat: the first layer started just under his breastbone, the middle layer resembled a tire around his body, and the bottom layer looked like an apron that passed down and hung below his crotch.

Sammy's mother was able to get a pittance from SSI, Social Security Insurance, because of her son's disability. Between that and her own Social Security income, Mrs. Wasserman could pay rent and put food on the table, but that was about it. The older Sammy and his mother became, the more pathetic was their situation. She would watch out her kitchen window as her son was being taunted by the neighborhood boys, tears streaming down her ruddy cheeks.

"I can't tie shoes. I have a hard time. I screw up," Sammy uttered, looking down at his feet, not making eye contact with any of them.

"Fuck you, Farquad. Don't make us kick your ass!" Allan yelled.

"I'm gonna tell your mother on you, that's what I'm gonna do, you just wait!" Sammy hollered back, finally exploding in his own version of the Stonewall Rebellion he'd recently seen on the news.

"You retard! That's your ass!" Bruce shouted.

Bookin' it, Sammy took flight as best he could toward his building with the five, long-haired, nineteen-year-olds in hot pursuit.

Sammy quickly waddled into the street and approached the stoop of his building, tripping on the first step but able to hold his balance enough so his girth didn't come crashing down onto the concrete pavement. He hurriedly hobbled up the steps, shaking uncontrollably, and made his way through the entrance door and into the marble vestibule yelling, "Mama! Mama!" as loud as he was able.

Allan, who was the fastest of his crew, bounded up the steps toward the front door of the building, just steps behind the hysterical Sammy.

Then it happened. The exact moment that would change Allan's life forever.

His adrenaline in full force as he neared closer to poor Sammy, Allan pushed with his right arm on the front door of the building, hitting the crystal glass sidelight instead of the wood door. He instantly saw his blood pouring down his arm, and the loud crinkle of the glass told Allan he had a major problem. Wide-eyed, and turning to look for his friends, Allan started to sweat profusely as the cortisol flowed through his body. The sting of the glass in his flesh was making him cower. Instinctively, he pulled his arm out of the pointed shards of glass, ripping his skin nearly down to his bone.

Blood was splattering everywhere as Allan went numb. Everything seemingly started to happen now in slow motion.

"Holy fuck! Holy Fuck!" one of the gang of five exclaimed.

"Jesus Christ, Allan, that's pretty bad!" Bruce uttered.

"What do I do? What do I do?" was all Allan could emit. The injured teen lowered his arm, the blood now pouring like an open faucet onto the worn, black, stoop steps and his All-Star sneakers. Allan felt a tingling in his stomach, dots coming up in front of his eyes. He felt himself about to pass out.

"Don't move, Allan. I got this!" Bruce commanded.

Bruce acted quickly, either from instinct or seeing what needed to be done from a movie or on television. He took out his handkerchief, put it around Allan's arm, just above his elbow and tied it with all his might into a makeshift tourniquet. The massive blood flow stopped instantly. Bruce likely saved his friend's life.

But Allan was in shock. He looked down at his arm as if it were not his. He looked at Bruce with doe eyes that pleaded, 'What now?'

"C'mon on…Montefiore," Bruce commanded.

Montefiore Hospital was a long, city block away on Bainbridge Avenue. Allan's crew ran, friends half-carrying their buddy to the front entrance of the hospital. They didn't even have the wherewithal to go around the corner to the emergency room entrance.

After much confusion, Allan was attended by several physicians and nurses who quickly stabilized his severely injured arm.

Karma...this is Karma! Allan whispered in his head, thinking of the torment he and his friends had laid upon the one they called Sammy the Retard.

He looked on sheepishly as the doctors gave him a mild sedative as he was still panicked from the harrowing experience. More than the pain though, Allan had a guilty conscience about Sammy and was feeling guilty.

While the staff at the nurse's station was going to try to get in contact with Mr. and Mrs. Fischer to approve the blood transfusion, the hospital's technicians wheeled Allan down for x-rays to determine just what extent the damage from the glass had done to the teen's arm and what type of surgery was going to be needed.

Allan, now in a mild stupor, knew his parents were at a Bar Mitzvah celebration on Long Island but could barely remember where the affair was being held. Someone on the staff started naming catering halls to him.

"That's it! That's where they are. Leonard's of Great Neck," Allan said, beginning to slur his words.

Hospital staff had the Fischers paged at Leonard's. They were told their son had severed his ulnar nerve.

"Dear, what does that mean?" Mrs. Fischer asked her husband.

"Like the doctor said, the ulnar nerve is one of the three main nerves which runs down from the spine to his hand. He's probably going to lose complete feeling in at least three of his fingers," Mr. Fischer replied to his worried wife. "C'mon, let's thank our hosts and get back home," Mr. Fischer said.

"Fucking Karma!" Allan whispered to himself again, just before the anesthesia totally kicked in for his surgery. Some guys coming home from the war didn't have it this badly, he thought as he drifted off.

The two-and-a-half hour operation was successful. While Allan was recuperating in his hospital room, the surgeon came in and met with him and his parents.

"Six weeks with this full cast, my boy. And another three weeks in a half cast. You will likely not regain feeling in your thumb through your middle finger so don't try to become a surgeon or a jeweler," the surgeon said.

"How many stitches did I get, Doc?" Allan asked.

"They always ask that. A full deck kid. Fifty-two. Now after the ninth week, you're going to need therapy. Your right arm will be all shriveled up and smaller than it was because of lack of use. We call that atrophy. You'll need to build up the muscle again. Oh, by the way, Allan, you kept saying Karma…just before you went under... and when you were in recovery. What's that all about?" the surgeon asked.

Allan's parents 'didn't know from Karma' as they said in the Bronx.

"Let's just say I was taught a life lesson today doctor, that's all," Allan murmured.

28 Years Later, 1997

Allan is now forty-seven years old, and he finds himself donating blood for a charity event at his daughter's school. He gave the required blood, had a cookie and some juice. He hears the chatter in the hallway of the children and, as he exits the building to drive home, he witnesses a group of young boys taunting another student outside. *Wow*, he thought to himself. If only those boys could know what could happen to them and most especially the effect it's having on the boy they are teasing. "Hey! Knock it off," he calmly tells them. The boys abide.

The next day the school nurse called Allan.

“Mr. Fischer, this is Alice the nurse over at the middle school. I have a matter I would like to discuss with you. Can you come in?"

"Certainly." *I hope nothing happened to that boy after I left the school yesterday. Why would the school nurse want me to come back in?* Allan wondered to himself.

As Allan drove to the school he was feeling pretty big about himself like he did when he had those quips when he and his buddies were younger. *I bet they want to hear how great I was and want to have an award night for me and give a speech on anti-bullying.* Allan's chest was beginning to puff up. He started to call his wife, but he decided to wait until he knew more.

The nurse took a deep breath.

"I called you in to inform you that your blood sample indicated you have Hepatitis C."

“What? What’s that?” Allan asked in alarm. "Is this a joke?" he asked looking around him for hidden cameras.

“I'm sorry to inform you, Mr. Fischer. Hepatitis C is a very serious disease and you need to see your doctor at once. It’s a blood virus,” Alice stated.

“A blood virus? How on earth do you get that? I'm not some crazy drug user."

“I know, Mr. Fischer; I'm sure you're not, but Hepatitis C, Mr. Fischer, can be contracted in a variety of ways. Yes, we see it with people who have shared needles, but also those who have gotten tattoos or body piercings with non-sterile instruments, or people who have had blood transfusions.”

Allan went pale. *Karma…again!* he thought.

“I...I had a transfusion... but that was when I was nineteen. Let’s see…that’s like twenty-eight years ago!” Allan said, panic starting to creep into his voice.

"Best thing to do is go see your doctor as soon as possible; they will run a second test on you. I don't want to alarm you, but testing for Hepatitis C back then wasn't as stringent as it is now. Only since 1992 has the FDA tested incoming donated blood for the hepatitis virus. I'm so sorry."

Allan went home and sat down on his sofa with the family medical encyclopedia and looked up Hepatitis C. What he read was not good. Allan hung his head as he remembered the day he and his crew terrorized Sammy Wasserman. A pang of guilt raged through his entire being. *How could I have been such an asshole? That poor man! What did he do to deserve us treating him that way? This is Karma all over again!* But then a sense of injustice ran through him as he thought, *but do I deserve this? n*ot even knowing whatever happened to old man Wasserman that same fateful day.

Allan made the phone call to his doctor's office. His doctor was in complete shock, and adamant. "Allan, you need to go through a battery of tests which we can do right here at Good Samaritan. We'll do a complete blood work-up including liver scans and a liver biopsy to see how this disease has affected your body."

Allan even had to take the uncomfortable liver biopsy twice because the technician didn't take a big enough piece the first time. *God damn it! More Karma! If I see that technician again he will know what Karma means, that stupid jerk,* Allan seethed, blaming everyone, even though he knew this was all his fault.

Immediate treatments of injections were necessary, according to the doctor, and so was the infectious disease specialist Allan had to go to, also.

"I should be smoking cigars with my buddies, but instead here I sit at this god damn hospital," Allan told an elderly man sitting next to him in the waiting room, "and I don't even have any symptoms!"

But he did. Allan did recall not being able to take a three mile walk with a friend one day. Only after a short while he had found himself fatigued. But that was it. No jaundice, no pain, nothing.

Reactions to the multiple injections that were needed for the Hepatitis C treatments in 1997 were pretty scary. Allan would lose his hair, feel like he had the flu all the time, and the lower extremity pain would really piss him off. He was advised to take the injections on a weekend so he wouldn't be too sick to go to work come Monday again. *Great*, Allan thought, *they want me to work my ass off all week, then on the weekends, when I'm supposed to be relaxing, I would have to feel like shit? What would be the point?* Allan wondered. *Why the fuck would I even do this when they tell me it may never cure me of this fucking disease anyhow? I don't want my obituary to read like some others do...that I 'lost my battle' to some stupid, fucking virus.*

A promotional on television caught Allan's eye. There was going to be a story about Hep C on the CBS evening news. Hepatitis C… The Silent Killer. This was serious stuff.

Allan decided not to take the treatments. His life was too busy; he couldn't take off work, but more importantly, something just told him not to do it. Allan's doctor wasn't happy, but he could not force his patient to do what he didn't want to do.

With the virtual "Sword of Damocles" hanging over his head waiting for the Hepatitis C to rear its ugly head, make him sick as a dog, and for sure shorten his life, Allan stuck to his convictions and received no treatment for his Hepatitis C.

Another 18 Years Later, 2015

Allan was now sixty-five years old and a much wiser man.

Allan oftentimes thought about poor Sammy Wasserman, a/k/a Farquad, a/k/a Sammy the Retard, and lamented how he was being punished for being an insensitive jerk.

Alone one day at home, Allan sat down on his deck with a cigar and had it out with himself. *How did I ever think I was better than this man? After what my family went through in the Holocaust, I go and treat another human being like this? I guess I deserve what's coming. As they say, 'what goes around comes around. 'Karma. I wish I could apologize to poor Sammy. I wonder what ever happened to him. I'm sure by now he's long gone. What a shame. I was so young and dumb. How do I ever forgive myself?*

Allan had finally grown up. He no longer laughed when he retold the story to his cigar pals. Those around him could see the sense of sadness in his eyes...not for what had happened to him, though, but for how he had treated another from his childhood.

A few days later a woman from Allan's doctor's office called. There was a new drug that had a ninety-six to ninety-nine percent cure factor. It was called Harvoni.

"Why on earth do you think this will work for me? I told you I wanted no such treatment; you haven't even told me about the side effects! Just let me be; I'm an old man now. Who cares?" Allan was sincere, but nearing martyrdom.

"Mr. Fischer, please hear me out. The doctor asked me to specifically call you for this treatment as you are a perfect candidate for it."

Allan calmed down and composed himself. "What does he mean, 'I'm the perfect candidate?'"

"Mr. Fischer, this new drug? It has only been proven to work on those who have Hep C, but have never had any previous treatment for it."

Allan could hardly believe his ears. *Good Karma? Happening to ME?*

"Go on, please," was all he could mutter. He could feel his throat starting to tighten as a gleeful feeling came in him.

"Mr. Fischer, this drug really works. It's not like the other treatment that was recommended before. There are really no major side effects. You take eighty-four pills. You get them from the manufacturer in three doses of twenty-eight pills. After each batch, we take your levels and see what is happening. But you need to apply for the company to approve you, and we need to check with your insurance carrier."

"I have to apply? I don't understand."

"Well, Allan…it cost ninety thousand dollars for the medication," the woman said.

"What? I don't have that kind of money," Allan laughed, more at himself for thinking good Karma had finally come his way.

"Let's see what your insurance company says. Looking at your file you do have excellent coverage. I'll call them for pre-approval. Sit tight."

"Miss, I've been sitting tight for forty-six years since the day I got that blood transfusion. A few days more certainly isn't going to matter," Allan blurted.

"I understand," was all she said.

"God damn, Karma!" This time he screamed it out loud. "How could one pathetic moment in my life haunt me for the rest of it? Sure, finally a cure and I can't fucking afford it," he said out loud to himself.

Now the days seemed to last forever as he waited for a response from the insurance company. *Christ, I could die from ten other things by the time they get back to me,* Allan thought to himself one morning while staring into the mirror at himself shaving. He tried to keep himself busy by visiting with his grandchildren.

A few days later, Allan received a call from a man with a bit of a southern accent. The man worked for the Hep C drug manufacturer in North Carolina. Allan had been approved for the drug, and his insurance would pick up all but one hundred fifty dollars for each twenty-eight pill packets.

"What? Say that again," Allan hollered, "Oh, my God!"

"Oh! Wait just one second sir, I see we also have a coupon we can apply. That will bring it down to fifteen dollars for each section. So, forty-five dollars out of pocket."

The original blood test before he started the pill regiment had shown Allan's viral count to be fifteen-million. Not bad, but not great. Actually, his numbers were borderline. Hep C was on the move in Allan's body.

He took the pills as prescribed, twenty-eight, then the blood test, three times until the pills were done.

The doctor called Allan at home on a Saturday.

"Allan, I have the results of your last blood test."

"How did I make out?" Allan asked. He held his breath.

"It's fifteen," the doctor pronounced.

"Shit, fifteen million again?"

"No Allan…fifteen…*just* fifteen. I'm delighted to say you no longer have Hepatitis C. It worked!"

Allan was speechless. Just like the day Allan's arm went through the glass in Sammy Wasserman's building and he felt dizzy, things started to go by very slowly now, too. It was as if he was not within his own body, but watching the whole scene from above. A surreal moment he retells in a hushed voice at the cigar bar nowadays.

Still on the phone, Allan closed his eyes so as not to cry tears of joy. Serendipitously, when he closed his eyes, he saw Sammy. Sammy Wasserman. His face, smiling at him, taped glasses and all.

THANKSGIVING

Eddie and I were walking through the Bronxdale Projects from the Monroe Houses a few days before Thanksgiving. Monroe, was where we lived since it was built in 1960. Ten, eight-story, and five, fourteen-story brick buildings, all surrounded by patches of grass and newly planted ash trees gave a parklike feeling to The New York City Housing Authority property. Bronxdale was older, darker, and dirtier, with twenty-five squat, closely laid out, six-story buildings. The grounds were no longer maintained. The once grass blotches were now mostly clay like dirt, that gave the project a worn and depressed look.

It was a cold and dreary November afternoon in the Bronx. Eddie and I wore our black dress leather jackets, which were pretty cool looking, and just enough to break the chilly breeze that signaled the upcoming winter. We both had black chino, un-cuffed pants like our entire group of friends in Monroe wore.

Bronxdale was a rough city project, one that was known for groups of mostly black teens who were notorious for not embracing strangers from other neighborhoods. Eddie is a dark-skinned Puerto Rican, six feet tall, athletically built with short jet-black hair. He could easily pass as a resident of the minority population of Bronxdale. My Italian, pale-olive complexion and five-foot seven thin build was a sure sign that we didn't belong. Our leather jackets were fair game.

In our low, black, Chuck Taylor Converse All-Star sneakers both of us were pretty fast on our feet. Eddie was two steps quicker than me, but I could hold my own. Neither of us were good with our hands and we relied on speed to get away if we were accosted. Why we were walking through Bronxdale on this particular day I can't recall but whatever it was, we weren't the kind of kids who would walk around the boundaries of the project to avoid a confrontation.

During school hours, we walked down this street, Beach Avenue, to get to Blessed Sacrament School together for the last four years. Never once were any of the students of Blessed Sacrament School approached nor was there any fear of getting jumped during daylight hours. In the late afternoon however, we were two gazelles, like prey roaming the Serengeti Plains. We walked briskly, but not too fast to show any fear. Our eyes and ears were used as defenses against any marauding gang that may pounce.

"Louie, we're not coming back this way in the dark. Too many buildings and shadows," Eddie blurted.

"Yep, we can go over to White Plains road and go back that way. More wide-open. This place is creepy," I observed.

As we passed the first Bronxdale building off Bruckner Boulevard, we both spotted a group of black kids that saw us at the very moment when we noticed them. Like a pride of lions, they bolted as one toward us.

"Run!" Eddie erupted. We took off down Beach Avenue, our adrenalin streaming through our bodies like the prey we were. The avenue was a wide, two-way street, lined with parked cars and very little moving traffic.

I was running on Eddie's heels, my un-buttoned jacket flapping in the wind, not helping my speed but I pushed through, kicking my legs like a track star.

"Get those motherfuckers!" was enough to make us break the world land speed record on concrete.

Our school and church was a long block and a short block away.

The group was five or six kids with kicking our asses and taking our leather as their only goal. They all wore high school basketball jackets, some still wearing gym shorts and high-top, white sneakers. Every neighborhood had their certain look. Ours advertised that we didn't belong.

Eddie was puffing his cheeks out as he did on the football or baseball field and I was breathing steadily into my nose and out of my mouth without even thinking about it. The danger was real and survival of the fittest was the order of the day.

These lions were fast, but our need to save our butts, and jackets gave us the slight edge we needed.

Instinctively, we knew not to wait to look for cars after the first block as we crossed over the intersection and onto the next block. We looked, but never stopped for any passing cars. If we stopped, even for a few seconds we were done for. I thought our pursuers would stop after the first block. No luck!

The gang followed us onto the short block. I could feel their presence just a few paces away but knew not to look back. If one of us tripped and fell they would be on us with a vengeance.

We came upon the small church. And old stone-like structure that had an almost gothic exterior.

I could hear the huffing and puffing of the pride right behind us.

Eddie was the first through the large front door, and in a second we were both in the safety and sanctuary of our church. Our pursuers wouldn't dare enter. They would wait. Maybe behind the parked cars on the street, maybe in a darkened alley, but they would surely wait.

"Holy shit that was close," Eddie puffed.

I put my hands on my thighs and bent over to catch my breath. Another block and they may have caught us. I remembered hearing about a kid who was stabbed outside the church on a summer night and wondered if that would have been my fate.

Inside the darkened church there were two elderly ladies lighting candles; their black kerchiefs fit tightly around their heads in deference to the sacred place. Halfway down in the left side pews there was a scruffy old man who was there every day. He would often pray out loud, his rosary beads wound around his hands, sometimes opening his arms in reverence to the massive crucified Christ that hung over the altar. He would cough up gobs of phlegm, and spit it into a large manila envelope, his gagging bouncing off the church walls.

To catch our breath, Eddie and I sat in the second row from the altar, mopping perspiration from our foreheads with my handkerchief.

“Man, Louie I thought my asthma was about to get me,” Eddie whispered. I had no idea Eddie had asthma. Eddie was a bit of a hypochondriac and always had some kind of pulled muscle or Ace bandage, tightly wrapped around his knee or arm. He was the best athlete among our crowd so we made allowances.

“I thought they had us for a minute,” I said. I could feel my adrenalin fading and my breathing became almost normal. I could still feel my heart pounding in my ears.

“How the fuck are we gonna get out of here?” Eddie asked.

“No idea. Maybe we just wait them out.”

“If I don’t get home at six-thirty my father will kick my Rican ass in for me.”

“Get ready for the beating because only a miracle will get us home on time.”

Suddenly, Sister Elizabeth, our teacher and Sister Irene Mary entered the church through the front side door where the ladies were lighting their votive candles.

“Oh, how nice. Look Sister, Edward and Louis are making a visit to our Lord. What good boys we have,” Sister Elizabeth blurted.

“Boys, would you like to help us deliver some packages to the needy families in the parish?” Sister Irene Mary asked.

“Yes, Sister!” we simultaneously replied.

“That’s wonderful. We were hoping some eighth graders would be around to help and the Lord sent you both here to us.”

Brownie points, I thought.

“Sister, may I call my mother and tell her we are helping? She will call Louis’ mother so they don’t worry.”

The next thing we were inside the darkened and mysterious one-story convent. Eddie called home and we were golden. Helping the sisters was like being in Jesus’ embrace.

In the antiseptic smelling hallway of the convent there were boxes of groceries, filled to the brim with turkeys, canned goods, fruits, and vegetables ready to be distributed to the poor. We were poor, too, but we didn't know it. Evidently, we were not as poor as other families in the parish. Eddie's and my family always had enough food. Our parents worked so we were able to pay the Catholic school tuition but not many extras. We both worked small odd jobs to help pay for our leather jackets and our sneakers and a few bucks for the Yankees bleacher seats during the baseball season, but that was about it. We had very few wants.

We were about to see what real poverty was about.

The parish had a Ford station wagon with faux wood sides and Eddie and I quickly loaded the car with the boxes. Sister Irene Mary drove and sister Elizabeth rode shotgun. The aroma of Ivory soap seemed to permeate the car. Cleanliness was close to Godliness, the nuns always said.

Eddie and I sat up straight in the back seat pretending to be two good boys who often made visits to the church when we were not commanded to be there. I glanced at Eddie a few times. He never came out of character. If he carried his rosary, I swear he would have whipped it out and pretended to be praying. I tried hard not to roll my eyes.

If Eddie had ever gone into acting he surely would have won an academy award.

The first stop was back into the bowels of the feared Bronxdale project. The nuns were with us so any roaming gang would not be an issue. We were in the lion's den but, the gangs were terrorizing the neighborhood elsewhere.

"Now, boys. Go up to apartment 3G. Knock politely on the door and announce that you are from Blessed Sacrament, with groceries." Sister Elizabeth commanded.

Eddie and I each took a box and entered the building. The smell of Puerto Rican cooking in the hallways reminded me that I was very hungry, but I knew it would be a while until I got home for a late supper.

I knocked on the brown, metal door a few times with no response. I looked at Eddie and shrugged my shoulders. "Now what?"

Eddie moved me aside and banged loudly on the door yelling out a bold, "Hello, anyone home?"

We could hear children in the apartment and a too loud television blaring.

Finally, a response. "Who?" A woman's voice.

"Blessed Sacrament Church with a package," I replied.

The sound of the security chain came from inside the door and we could hear the unbolting of a door-to-floor police lock.

A young, black mom, in a flowery house dress opened the door with her hair all askew as if she were sleeping.

"What's this about?"

"Holiday food from Blessed Sacrament Church," Eddie announced.

"Leave it!"

The door slammed in our faces. She started yelling at the kid to be quiet. So much for gratitude.

We left the boxes and shrugged to each other. Back down to the station wagon.

"All good?'

"Yes, Sister," we both replied.

The next stop was a Puerto Rican family a few blocks away in another look-alike building. The musty hallway was totally dark. The overhead light bulbs were all missing, evidently taken by the tenants for light in their own apartments.

The door was answered on the first knock.

"Ay Dios, mio!" The mother of a clan kids exclaimed. The kids all ran to the door. The sound of Tito Puente, loud and rhythmic, escaped from the apartment and flooded the narrow hallway.

The kids were jumping up and down trying to look into the boxes of groceries. The woman began to cry. Eddie and she spoke Spanish to each other as we brought the boxes into the stark apartment and through into the kitchen.

I noticed tears in Eddie's eyes. These were his people. The diminutive woman was gushing and enormously grateful for the holiday food. She quickly opened her purse offering us some coins as a tip. Eddies lips were quivering as we both raised our hands disallowing any gratuity. I understood very little Spanish but enough to know that she was blessing Jesus and us for the gifts of food for her family. Eddie and I said nothing to each other on the way down in the elevator to the car, and the safety of the good sisters.

On to the third and last family. Another project building inside the notoriously dangerous and foreign Bronxdale projects. Three unsavory characters were loitering inside the urine smelling vestibule. They looked at us and peeked outside seeing the nuns inside the Ford. We were free to pass.

Our stop was to a first-floor apartment, so the rough looking thugs, who all wore black skull caps, were able to watch the proceedings.

I knocked on the door, politely as instructed by Sister.

"Who is there, please?"

"Blessed Sacrament Church with packages," Eddie responded.

A tall, very pale white man, his eyes sunken and dark opened the door. His eyes were rolling up into his skull. He was obviously blind.

"Good evening. May I ask what this is about?" he queried.

"We have two boxes of groceries for Thanksgiving," I proclaimed.

"Well, isn't that wonderful. Please come in…please." He opened the door wide and Eddie entered first.

"The apartment was dark. The family had no need for light. The two blond kids, both wearing blue, plaid shirts and gray pants, and the mother, her hair matted and her house dress wrinkled, were also blind.

There was an old, worn sofa and one folding chair, the kind you would see at the church bingo hall, in the small living room. An old, brown radio was on a wooden stand. It was on a news channel bringing the world into their home.

A black braille typewriter on a gray metal stand, with a folding chair in front, stood aside from the small kitchen table. Braille paper was in the typewriter package, a few pages had spilled onto the black tile floor.

"Children, come and see what the church has sent to us. It's wonderful…truly a blessing," the dad said.

I took the turkey from the box. "Here is a nice, fat turkey," I announced.

The kids began to feel the turkey. They touched every inch of the bird. They both had the same eyes as their father. Their eyes seemed to be covered by a film and their heads bobbed in circles as they examined the turkey.

The mom, also blind but not totally, took a large can of yams from the box. She brought it within an inch of her eyes and announced what it was.

"Look, everyone. Yams. I can make these with some brown sugar and a bit of maple syrup."

The kids and the dad rolled the can in their hands, all three smiling widely.

They smelled the apples and the rest of the produce, feeling everything.

I was utterly speechless. Eddie was quietly crying, wiping the tears away from with his hands. Between the Puerto Rican family and this blind family, his emotions spilled over. I looked away so not to embarrass my friend.

The father felt with his arms for his children and wife. They all gathered in a huddle and were filled with joy.

"We need to say a prayer," the dad announced.

"Bless us our Lord, and these Thy gifts. You have made us truly thankful for your generosity. Bless these boys who have brought these packages to us on this cold night. Bless their families, too, O, Lord. And, thank you, Lord, for our lives together."

"Boys, can we offer you some juice or milk?" the mother offered.

We made our excuses and thanked them wishing them a happy Thanksgiving. We passed the three thugs in the hallway who were passing a refer to one another.

The sisters drove us back to the Monroe Houses thanking us for helping. Eddie and I knew they were sincere and we would be remembered by all of the nuns in the convent, for our good work.

When I got home. I tried to explain the families that we visited. When I got to the story of the blind family I started to cry. Being a tough kid, in a tougher neighborhood, tears never came easy for me. My mother hugged me, something she didn't often do when I hit my teen years.

From that night 'til today, fifty-five years later, I've always tried to be generous to those who are less fortunate than me. When I go back to the old neighborhood, some of the local panhandlers are not often well accepted. "Get a job," among other, harsher words are said to these desperate people. Me? I always keep fives and tens in my pocket for the street people. Some of them recognize my car. I see them smile, most toothless or deformed, when they see me, knowing a few bucks are coming their way. Their smiles and handshakes mean a lot to me. After all, I could have been them except for a bit of good timing, good luck, or if you believe in it…the grace of God. These people on the streets are my church.

There's a difference between being poor and being desperate. I had no idea when I was growing up that we were basically poor people. My parents didn't have a savings or checking account. But, I could recognize those who were *desperate,* like the families we visited that long-ago November night in the projects.

DOLLAR SIGN

The Catholic Church was in its salad days. Angelo Giuseppe Roncalli, Pope John XXIII, had called the Second Vatican Council. We prayed daily for His Holiness' success. John Fitzgerald Kennedy was President of the United States. Not just president but the first, Irish-Catholic president in our nation's history. We prayed daily for his success, also. The mass was still in Latin and nineteen new churches were completed in the United States that year. Money was flowing into the Vatican like a torrent. We prayed for the money not to stop. A song called *Sign* came out in the 70s. The words are: "Sign, sign, everywhere a sign..." With the Catholic Church, the only sign they knew was the Almighty Dollar sign.

IS THERE HEAVEN?

Is there heaven?
Or simply a nice place to stay
or just a memory
that will last for eternity?
Each one of us
may get to choose,
the best moment of our lives,
to re-live over and over,
not with boredom but bliss.
We choose from a snapshot
of our own memory,
best time, place, feeling, people.
A picnic in the mountains,
a holy place that we revere,
a battlefield with the smell of death
in victory.
A ballgame with dad.
A hole-in-one with my boy.
The favorite lover moment.
The day at the beach.
At the lake.
Pebble Beach?
Orchard Beach?

Grandma's kitchen,
Mom's smile.
Under a palm tree,
A Cuban. Not a person.
That perfect dinner.
The voice of a friend.
A salami sandwich,
on seeded hard bread.
Holding hands.
The kids' graduations,
The grandkids recognizing you
for the first time.
A stickball game,
the fruit man,
the ice cream guy,
the one that peddled the ice-box,
and the one with the red-tiled roof,
the aroma of the best pizza ever,
your favorite music,
at the perfect volume.
THE kiss.
And nowhere,
and I know this for sure,
Will money or things
Be counted

or considered?

Nope.

Choose yours.

PAYING IT FORWARD

Barry Kaplan, a handsome young man with blond hair, blue eyes and a cherubic, engaging smile, was just eighteen in 1984 when he became a student at Johnson and Wales University in Providence, Rhode Island. He went up to the famous school in New England to study the culinary arts, and the hospitality business.

A Jewish kid from New City in Rockland County, a suburban town, just thirty minutes from New York City as the crow flies, Barry, found himself in a difficult situation; he needed to pay his own tuition and expenses. His parents, old school Bronx refugees didn't have the where-with-all, so Barry was determined to do what he needed to do to make a better life for himself. Wanting to stay in a business he would be studying, Barry found a job in a Greek restaurant in rough and tumble East Providence. His boss, the restaurant's owner Dimitri, gave him a job as a cook, teaching him how to make and plate Greek specialties. Barry worked long hours following Dimitri's family recipes from the old country. After a couple of months, Dimitri called Barry into his small, cluttered office just off the kitchen.

"I have great news, Barry. My younger brother is coming from Greece to stay with me and work here," Dimitri announced.

"Very nice!" Barry responded.

"You will become the dishwasher and my brother will cook."

"Um, sir, I don't understand. I can wash dishes with the best of them, but this is like a demotion. They don't really teach dishwashing at the school," Barry protested.

"It will be fine. You'll see. My brother is your age, and you will like him. Maybe teach him some English."

"I'll teach him Yiddish if you want, but that will be an extra charge."

Soon, the brother came to East Providence and Dimitri and he sat at the bar drinking while Barry did both the cooking, and cleaned the dishes. After a few nights of this, Barry went to Dimitri.

"Look, Dimitri. I'm doing everything now and for the same amount of money, so I'm sorry, but I have to quit," Barry lamented. Barry needed the job but knew he would find another restaurant gig in short order, and he also needed to preserve his dignity.

"No..no, Barry. Here, take this. You work good, and I like you," Dimitri said. He handed Barry a fifty-dollar bill.

"Okay, but I will expect this all the time for the added work," Barry said waving the money in front of Dimitri's solemn face.

Dimitri agreed to the raise, but Barry then, after a while, found he was wearing himself down. Barry worked until after the joint closed at eleven at night and had to study and make class by eight every morning.

After some time, one of the old regulars in the Greek restaurant, Paul Reed, made Barry a better offer.

"I've been watching how hard you work here, Barry, and I want you to come work for me. Look, I'm in the insurance business and also opened a place called Pub Dennis. It's a chain I took a franchise with, and it's a mess. I'm confident you can help," Paul stated.

"It's a deal," Barry said, without even asking about the pay. With that, Barry left Dimitri and the spanakopita to work the pub for Paul.

After three weeks, Barry had the front and back of the house at Pub Dennis at peak performance. The young, Jewish kid from New York got rid of a few deadbeats Paul had working for him. Barry got the food and booze ordering humming perfectly, and the joint was showing a great profit. Barry was being paid well. He ran the busy kitchen and oversaw the barmaids. Here he was, now just shy of nineteen years old, telling workers who were much older than he was, how to do their jobs. His humility and infectious smile made it easy for people to want to work for him. Paul was thrilled with the arrangement, and Barry was paying for tuition and saving his money for a car.

One day, before the pub opened, Paul called Barry and told him to come into work that day wearing a suit and tie.

"Ok, boss."

“Nice suit. You are now the general manager. Hire a chef, and run the place like it’s your own,” Paul said.

"What? Ok!" A rush of excitement filled Barry to his core. Barry had no idea how he fell onto such luck, but was thrilled to get the promotion and start getting to know even more of the regulars at 'his' place.

Barry now walked around, chatting it up at each table, welcoming the patrons, patting them on the back. His smile and youthful appearance also brought in a younger crowd. Waiters, dressed in black slacks and lavender shirts and food runners in all white pants and black, golf shirts, were buzzing like bees in and out of a hive. Bus boys were fast to clean up the tables so they could reach a three time per night turnover goal. The phones were ringing off the wall with take out orders and reservations.

Most of the crowd were young, college students, and an equal amount of white and blue collar workers. Then, there were the older ones with names like Vito, Carlo, Shorty, Petie, Little Petie, and Louie Cheese Balls who came into the joint daily, like a religion. And of course, there was Roger. Roger, Barry soon noticed, seemed to be the boss of this nattily-dressed crew, all of whom had slicked-backed hair, wore silk suits, silk ties, Italian loafers, silk socks, and finished off with custom-made shirts and gold cufflinks.

The only thing Barry thought was strange was Roger’s name. *What kind of Italian name was Roger?* Barry thought to himself.

After a few months, Paul, the joints owner, having still been observing Barry and whispering his name to Roger more than once, told Barry the place was now completely his...lock, stock, and barrel. Paul had decided to relocate to Boca Raton, Florida, deciding to tell Barry he was just better suited solely for the insurance business and not the pub business. All Paul wanted was the franchise to be paid and a few dollars sent to him each month. Barry was all in. Young Barry had recently started smoking cigars and had gotten a real feel and taste for the business.

Barry's place became the official hangout for Roger and his crew. Roger had a phone installed on the bar that he used for the Greyhound races, horse races, college basketball games, football games, anything that could be gambled on.

Barry never gave a bill to Roger or his crew. They left more than enough cash for him at the end of each night.

One night, after closing, with piles of cash being counted on the bar by Roger's guys, Roger called Barry to the side.

“Jew Boy!” That’s what they called Barry with all affection intended. “I don’t like how you're dressing." Barry was shocked. "What is it with this dark, sports jacket?” Roger said, handling the lapel of Barry's jacket, "And the tan pants? Forgetaboutit! And those motherless, brown, fuckin' shoes. Tomorrow, you hear me? Tomorrow, youse go to Providence Tailors. They will know you are around me. See Sal. He will fix you up,” Roger whispered. "Now repeat after me...Providence Tailors."

"Providence Tailors. Got it." Barry instinctively was looking around for Paul, but the old owner was nowhere to be found, him having moved to Florida.

As instructed, the very next day, Barry went to the tailor, saw Sal, and walked out with a pair of black, alligator loafers, a gorgeous, black suit, three cotton shirts, three ties, and two sets of cuff links. Sal said the bill was all taken care of.

"Well! Look at Jew Boy," Little Petie announced later that day as Barry walked into Pub Dennis, smiling from ear to ear, his hair slicked back and corrected with an ounce of Brylcreem Hair Cream.

"Now, you'se look like somebody special!" Louie Cheese Balls proclaimed with a huge smile.

Every member of Roger's crew shook Barry's hand, patted him on the back, and stuffed cash into the lapel pocket of his new, shiny suit. Roger sat at the bar, beaming with the pride of a Godfather.

Pub Dennis was right next to the Civic Center, in a neighborhood which was seedy, to say the least. When a sporting event was held, the Pub was packed with all sorts of characters. Gamblers, hookers, second story men, cops, both legit and on the take, you name it. Barry never had to concern himself with bouncers or security guards. The word was out that Pub Dennis was a protected place and that was that, but Barry didn't know that.

He did, however, know he now had enough money to buy himself a new Nissan Sentra…in cash. The night he took the car to Pub Dennis, there were no parking spots in front of the joint, so he parked around the corner. When he came in, Roger asked where his new car was parked and Barry told him. Roger got up off his barstool, took a look out of the Pub's window, and saw a car parked smack dab in front of the place that he wasn't familiar with.

"Hey! Who has the blue Plymouth outside?" Roger announced.

An unsuspecting diner at the far end of the bar claimed the vehicle.

Pointing to him with the hand that held his cigar, he said, "Be a nice guy and move it. The Jew Boy needs the spot." It was not a request but an order. No questions were asked, not a word was spoken. The patron immediately got up and headed outside with Barry following to get to his new Nissan and park the car right out in front in the prime spot. He exited his car standing a little taller, feeling like a movie star from all the attention.

And there it was. Roger watched from the window. Barry's Nissan was now parked between a line of Cadillac Devilles and Lincoln Town Cars, nestled like a baby elephant around its herd. The crew congratulated Barry when he came back in as if he just bought a Bentley convertible.

This is all the Jew Boy could afford, but he had worked hard for it. Roger and his boys were very proud of Barry's accomplishment, and he was very proud of himself.

One night, toward the end of the second semester of Barry's sophomore year, Roger slowly put the telephone down, turned down the portable transistor radio from where he obtained his racing and sports results, and glared at Barry, then gave him a quizzical look.

“Ah, Jew Boy. How's school?” Roger queried.

“Not bad, Roger. I have finals coming up.”

“So, when do you study, kid?”

“Not too much time for that with this place.”

“Go to your car and get those books,” Roger commanded, “Right now!"

Three minutes later, there was Barry, his books opened on top of the bar, while he was being quizzed by the two Peteies, Louie Cheese Ball, Vito, and two or three other wiseguys. Barry was questioned on recipes, accounting practices, wine pairings, and the like. Roger wasn't going to let the Jew Boy fail on his watch.

Barry had a hot date one evening. He was trying to score with a classmate and he asked her to dinner at a good Italian restaurant in Providence. He took the night off and told the barmaid where he was taking his gal. The barmaid told Roger that Jew Boy was going to Andino's, a fancy place with linen tablecloths. Not a joint many Johnson and Wales students could afford.

"Let me order for you. It will be my pleasure and my honor to serve such a good-looking couple," Andino's owner offered.

Barry and his date shrugged their shoulders as if to say, *Why not?*

To this day, Barry said he never ate that much food in his life. Wines the Jewish kid couldn't even pronounce were served with each course. Barry worried about the bill. There was no bill. Everything was compliments of Andino's. He insisted Barry leave no tip.

Barry's date was wide-eyed from the entire evening. Did he score? Barry never said if he did or not when he got back to his own haunts, but the look on his face was telling.

The night after, Barry was closing up the restaurant after having done some last-minute paperwork. He still had to bring the cash from the day's register to the bank deposit slot, and it was late. Barry patted his pocket where he kept the Beretta .22 caliber pistol Roger had given him. The registration numbers had been scraped off. The gun was never loaded, but Roger thought it was a good idea for Barry to show that bulge in his jacket. Barry never really needed his own protection because the locals knew he was always being guarded and was a protected species.

With the turn of the key, Barry slammed the door shut, and at the same time, an ear-deafening bang happened, startling Barry like he never experienced in his twenty young years. An immediate second bang had Barry scrambling to get back inside with the money. He reached in his pocket for his cell phone to text Roger. He had always been taught by the crew to say as little as possible to strangers and to mind his own business, and seeing as it sounded like the shots came from the Irish bar next to Pub Dennis, it was easy for him to be a good student. His heart was racing as he waited to see what happened before he attempted to leave the building again.

As Barry approached Pub Dennis the next day, he saw the street filled with flashing lights from the police cars and vans. Sure enough, the owner of the Irish bar was whacked the night before. Shot twice in the head. He was left where they found him.

Holy shit! Barry thought. His parking spot was taken, so he parked a block away and walked inconspicuously to his pub trying to look like your average college student, fancy clothes aside.

As Barry unlocked the door, detectives swarmed him, asking questions for over an hour. What time did he close the pub? Had he seen or heard anything? They tried to find out if the Jewish kid with the New York accent knew why anyone would want to see his competitor dead. Barry knew, heard, nor saw anything.

Roger and his crew came in early that day but said nothing about the murder to Barry, but they knew from their cop friends that Jew Boy said not a word to help out with the investigation. Barry was now even stronger in Roger's eyes, if that were even possible.

The year flew by and Barry invited his parents to come up to the school from Rockland County and go to Pub Dennis for supper. Roger saw to it that the hookers and undesirables which frequented the Pub all knew the place was off limits that particular evening. Roger and his crew laid low that night, going to a joint they knew across town. The Kaplans were none-the-wiser of the company their boychick, Barry was keeping.

Just before graduation in the spring, Dimitri walked into Pub Dennis. The Greek had heard about the knockout bartender who worked at the Pub, and he was going to put the moves on her. Dimitri did know Barry worked there but had no idea he ran the place.

The Greek pulled out all the stops on the barmaid, giving her every line he had ever known and then some. She was uncomfortable with the persistent remarks the Greek was making. When Barry came into Pub Dennis, he could tell what was going on immediately. He approached Dimitri, who was stunned to see the young man so dressed.

"Look who is in my place! Dimitri, old pal. I suppose you came here to wash the dishes for me?" Barry asked cooly. He was, however, loud enough so the entire Pub could hear his words.

Dimitri was furious and made a move toward Barry.

Six guys stood up. "Excuse me? You, Valentino! You got a problem washing the kid's dishes?" Roger bellowed.

The Greek threw some bills on the bar and fled Pub Dennis like it was under nuclear attack.

Barry was loved. He was family. East Providence still remembers the graduation party Roger and the boys threw for the Jew Boy. Barry then gave the keys to the guy who Paul hired to replace him and would now take over.

The mob guys never asked Barry to stay. They never asked for him to get into their group or be part of their life. Jew Boy would always and forever be the student from New York who they watched over and protected.

Barry, many years later, can't even have a plate of ziti with vodka sauce without thinking of Roger and the boys. Each time, a wide smile and a silent, *thank you* is offered up by Barry.

THE TWO LADIES

It was one of those hot Bronx days in July where if we hung around the project, trouble was sure to find us.

A few of the guys decided to go to Orchard Beach to beat the heat and dodge the floating condoms we called white eels.

To me, the bay water was never appealing, or all that clean, so I decided to find some of our crew to go to Yankee Stadium to see a day game. I think the Bombers were playing the Orioles, but who they were playing became unimportant. Only two of the boys wanted to go; Dominick and Eddie. Eddie was a regular for the games and Dominick wasn't punished by his strict parents, for a change. Not that my or Eddies parents weren't tough as nails, it was just that Dom's mom and dad were on the right side of insane.

Frankly, the thought of roasting in the right field bleachers wasn't too tempting either, but anytime we could see Mickey Mantle and company play ball, we scrounged up the money and got to the stadium. Besides, if some great event like a no hitter or a Mantle grand-slam, walk-off homer happened while we were there, we would have bragging rights over the beach goers for the remainder of the summer.

The price was right, too. Fifteen-cents, in each direction, by elevated train and subway from Soundview Station on the Pelham Line. Sometimes a kind collector would let us use our school transit pass after hours and the ride was a freebee. Seventy-five cents for bleacher seats and another quarter for a couple of sodas. Most of the money was kept in our sneakers in case we got jumped. You could hand over a dime but never nothing. That's how you got your ass kicked for sure.

We usually wanted to get to the Stadium a few hours before the game to hawk a few player autographs and fantasize about meeting a couple of girls to spend the afternoon and maybe get a phone number. Ball player signatures were available but girls never were. I now know that any respectable girl in 1964 would be going to general admission or box seats to meet guys who had a few bucks rather than us ghetto snipes in the bleachers. Oh, well.

Dominick had to help his sister do some mandatory chores for their mom, like Windex and clean all the windows in the apartment, so we planned to get to the stadium just a bit before game time. Oh well again.

The train was always on time except for equipment failure or a jumper. This particular day things on the Pelham Line were running smoothly.

Me, Dominick and Eddie wore our street uniforms at all times during the summer. Black chino pants, low black, Converse All-Star Chuck Taylor sneakers with black crew socks, and a white, crew-neck tee shirt. Dom wore a 'guinea-t' muscle shirt. That was appropriate and permissible.

I wasn't the best at using the trains because I never really paid attention, and just followed the guys who knew. What I did know is we needed to take the train to 125th Street in Harlem, go downstairs and transfer to another train that went back up to the Bronx and the Yankee Stadium station. It's the D train but I wasn't really sure. I should have paid better attention.

So, the three of us make the first leg of the trip up to Harlem. My pulse began to quicken because, in those days, there were very few whites at 125th Street. Not that the projects had no blacks, but in those days, Harlem was not too used to seeing two Italian kids, who stuck out like sore thumbs. Eddie is Puerto Rican so it was basically me and Dom who were getting the hairy eyeballs. One guy asked me if he could "hold a nickel." I told him we got jumped at the Cypress Avenue station and wiped out. Somehow, he bought it.

Now the trip got real interesting.

Instead of going upstairs to change trains, don't ask me to recall how it happened, we wound up on the sidewalk of 125th Street. Not a good move at all. We ran smack into what I could only call a mini-riot. Don't ask me how it got started or when it ended. All I remember is people were screaming and running in every direction. I saw one guy throw a grocery store carriage through a plate glass window of a sporting goods store. It was sheer bedlam.

We tried to head back into the not so safety of the subway. A swarm of unfriendly-looking black guys were crowding the stairs, some of them pushing on each other. The fight was spreading quickly, and it was no place for us to be.

"Louie, what the fuck?" Dom hollered.

"You and your Yankee game! We should have gone to Orchard. This is bullshit," Eddie blurted.

"We have one shot. We need to hail a cab," I pronounced, as if I had ever hailed a cab in my life up to that point. I saw my father do it a few times but I could never do that two fingers in the mouth whistle thing he did.

There were only yellow cabs in those days and they were not about to stop for three punk teens in the middle of a street war in Harlem. As a matter of fact, not one cab even stopped for the red lights. I looked across the street and the guy who asked me for the nickel was looking at me waving my arm like crazy for a cab. He now surmised that we had money and was looking to make his move and pounce on us. He started dodging the speeding cars to get across the street. All I could think was, *Oh shit!*

If I had doubted that God existed, it was at this moment that I rejected atheism.

Miraculously, a yellow cab screeched to a halt right in front of us and the rear passenger door swung open. A black Muslim woman got out of the cab quickly. Well I think she was a Muslim by the way she dressed. She wore a white gown and headdress. The three of us project waifs literally dove into the taxi.

"What the hell are you kids doing here?" the beefy, white cabbie queried. "Youse are gonna get ya selves all three killed!" He wasted no time and peeled out from the curb.

"We were trying to get the stadium and we screwed up on the trains," I stated.

"You must be three idiots. Okay, I'll take you there for a buck."

"How about fifty-cents, we don't have enough to get into the game," I implored.

"Sure, next time know where the hell you're going kid."

"Next time I'm watching the game on channel eleven."

Dominick farted. Either from fear of what just happened or from the beans and macaroni Mrs. Police made for lunch.

The cabby raced uptown toward the stadium. I felt the bile rise into my throat as I've always suffered from car sickness. I put my head back and closed my eyes, willing the puke to stay down in my stomach.

Finally, 161st Street and River Avenue. The massive Yankee Stadium looked like heaven to me.

I paid the cabbie and we all three thanked him for saving our lives. He mumbled something about idiots again and was gone in an instant.

We could hear the crowd erupt to a play. The game had started.

The three of us started running fast toward the bleacher entrance.

"Hey you. You three…stop!" a uniformed cop hollered.

"Jesus Christ, now what?" Eddie begged.

We walked toward the officer not knowing what we had done to get his attention.

"You…you Italian?" The cop signaled me out.

"Yeah. What did we do?"

"Nothing at all. Here, take these tickets. Enjoy the game. We take care of our own."

I looked down at the four, field-box seat tickets in my sweaty hands. All I could see was the price. $3.50.

"Holy shit…Thanks-a-lot!" I exclaimed. The cop smiled and pointed to the nearby entrance.

Sitting in box seats was a brave new world for us. It was unimaginable. Field-level! That very phrase was made for other people, not those of us who lived in New York City Housing Authority projects.

The ticket taker guy actually said, "Thank you, enjoy the game."

On that first level, the grass seems to pop in a majestic green that reminded me of something royal, something way more special than peering out from the far away bleachers.

Walking through the tunnel entrance and into the arena gave me goosebumps that would not quit. My senses were overwhelmed.

Seeing the façade that encased much of the stadium from ground level, me, Dom, and Eddie must have looked like those country bumpkins, who stare up at the office buildings and skyscrapers when they visit New York City for the first time.

"Let's find our seats," Eddie uttered.

Having stashed the one unused ticket into my pocket for posterity and to show the Orchard Beach mongrels some proof of the event of a lifetime, I looked down at my ticket stub for the section number.

A blue-blazered, uniformed usher who smelled like stale cigars and warm beer came up upon us with his hands pushing out from his shoulders.

"C'mon boys you gotta go back up top, to general admission… youse know better, c'mon, c'mon." He started to guide us back down the tunnel when I stopped him.

"Look…we have tickets!"

He took the stub from my hand like I had leprosy.

"Where'd jew get dese tickets, kid?"

"Never mind…my cousin is a cop in the four-four. He gave them to us for my birthday," I pronounced.

"I dunno…we don't get many kids like youse down here."

"Okay, Einstein, just point out where the seats are, will ya?" Dom erupted.

The Yankees were about to get up to the plate for the bottom of the first inning. I looked up to see the Yankee leadoff hitter, Bobby Richardson waiting for the opposing pitcher to get through with his warm ups.

"Okay, follow me but if youse are pulling sometin', I swear to Christ…"

We had no idea where our seats were. As the usher walked down the aisle toward the seats, he kept turning around and looking at us incredulous that three, gutter rats would be sitting in the front row next to the Yankee dugout.

We get to the seats and Einstein the usher, puts his hand into a velvet like mitten, opens the three, folded seats and wipes them clean. In those days, the fans in field box seats would hand a coin as a tip to the usher. Einstein was crude and dumb but he was smart enough to know he had no shot of seeing even a penny from the likes of us.

"I don't want no trouble out of the tree a youse. I kick you asses onto a hun sixty furst the furst sign of anything," Einstein muttered.

"Thank you, sir," Eddie said in his best Catholic school deference voice.

I was just too awestruck to respond. Dominick was busy looking at a blonde with a rocket bra sitting behind us and to the left to care less where our seats were.

Suddenly, a security guard and an usher were escorting two older women to the empty seats next to us. They could have been forty or ninety. Any one over forty seemed old to me then so all I thought was, they were old ladies.

The misguided product of parochial schools, we were taught to be polite, especially when we were sitting in the front row at Yankee stadium, which was never before or since.

"Hello, young men," the one lady announced. The other one smiled and gave us a short, wave hello. The older of the two sat right next to me on my right.

Eddie stood up and almost curtsied. "Good afternoon, ladies," he sprouted, to which they both smiled. He was like Eddie Haskell on Leave it to Beaver when adults were around.

"Would you cut it out, Rico Suave," I whispered to Eddie. He always had this good boy look on his face when he needed it and I cracked up laughing.

"ATTENTION PLEASE…LADIES AND GENTLEMEN." Bob Sheppard the venerable, long-time Yankee Stadium public address announcer interrupted the buzzing crowd.

"I direct your attention to the field box seats next to the Yankee dugout. Please give a warm Yankee Stadium welcome to, MRS. BABE RUTH and MRS. LOU GHERIG."

At the sound of those two immortal names the crowd erupted like a volcano of applause and cheers. For the first time in my life, I felt the presence of greatness.

I'm sitting next to Mrs. Babe Ruth!

The two ladies, Mrs. Ruth, was dressed in a trim blue dress with a blue hat that seemed a bit out of date, while Mrs. Gehrig wore a beige dress and a white hat and white gloves. They were a picture of both elegance and fame. They stood and waved to the crowd making certain they both turned to every section for the all fans. It seemed like the applause lasted forever. I stood to clap with the rest of the crowd but was so dumbfounded to be sitting next to such fame that I was numb. Eddie kept hitting me in the side with his bony elbow. Dominick couldn't care less. He just kept watching the blonde, now jiggling cutely as she clapped.

I looked out onto the hallowed field and the entire Yankee team was out of the dugout, in a sea of pinstripes, applauding these two ladies. And there he was, the Mick, beaming his schoolboy smile and clapping like everyone else. I wondered if he saw me standing next to Mrs. Ruth? Maybe he thought I was a relative of the Babe?

The crowd settled down and the bottom of the second inning got underway.

It took a lot of nerve and I practiced my words wanting to make sure I didn't stutter.

"You were actually married to the Babe?" I asked.

"Indeed, I was, young man."

"What was he like? I mean, it must have been amazing to be his wife."

"Everything you ever hear about Babe will likely be true. Let me tell you he was larger than life. And he loved the fans."

"I never saw him play. He was gone before I was even born."

"Too bad. It was a special thing to see him round the bases."

Mrs. Ruth was very friendly and comfortable to talk with. Her face brightened and her eyes twinkled when she spoke of her great husband. Mrs. Gehrig didn't exude that kind warmth. She seemed removed from the moment, almost like a teacher who was about to mark a test paper. Perhaps she was in deep thought as she looked out on the field. Maybe she saw her Lou at first base in her mind's eye. Or maybe she was tired of being second to the Babe.

"Where did you and the Babe live, Mrs. Ruth?"

"Right on Riverside Drive. You know, I've never emptied his clothes closet. He's gone a good sixteen years and it seems like he is still here with us."

"Wow!" is all I could muster.

The game I was watching was no longer important to me. I was next to the woman that the "Sultan of Swat", the great "Bambino," called his wife.

I had a small note pad and Bic pen in my back, pant pocket in case we ran into one of the ball players going to their cars after the game. I mustered up the courage to ask for the two ladies' autographs.

"Would you mind signing for me?" I asked loud enough for both of these famous women to hear. I focused on Mrs. Gehrig because something told me she wouldn't sign. But she did.

Mrs. Gehrig reached for my pad and smiled.

"My name is Louis," I uttered.

"Ahh, what a coincidence, that's my favorite name."

She wrote on my pad and handed it to Mrs. Ruth, who smiled and signed.

When Mrs. Ruth handed back the pad and pen to me I saw her signature first.

Claire Ruth. Just her name. I stared at it for a few seconds and then looked at Mrs. Gehrig's page.

To Louis, All my best wishes, Eleanor Gehrig.

Eddie grabbed the pad from me and stared at the signatures.

"Holy shit, Louie…holy shit!" Eddie whispered.

After the inning ended and the Mick fanned on three pitches, the two ladies gathered their pocketbooks.

"Well, young man, it's time that we left. It was a pleasure to meet you," Claire Ruth said.

The two women stood and left. I stood too, in awe of the moment.

The rest of the game was uneventful. I don't remember who won or lost. All I knew was that I was at the door of immortality and I liked the feeling.

On the train, back to the Bronx I flashed back to the scene on 125th Street, the gruff cab driver and the nearly pukey ride, the Italian cop, Einstein the usher, and how all the universe aligned to make the most incredible moment of my young life.

POEM TO ANCESTORS

I wrote this poem in Palermo in memoriam to my ancestors.

DOROTEA

In the harbor, the sailboat masts
Keep time like metronomes
To the tinkling of the piano keys.
I see across the harbor
In my minds eye...
A woman with three very small children
Clinging to her peasant dress
Boarding the ship
With the huddled masses.
I whisper, "Grazie, Nonna,
For the good voyage
You gifted us."

THROUGH OLD EYES

I can see how people look at me.

A stout, older man, with lots of gray hair.

Experienced.

The hunch of time that has gradually caught up.

A grandfatherly man with telling eyes,

Pleasant smile, waiting for his turn.

I look at them through eyes at their age.

The pretty teen I see through my adolescent memory.

She gets ready for the brave new world in anticipation,

I divert my glaze, leaving her at peace.

The bride, I view her as the groom does.

Ready for a new life.

Momentarily happy, awaiting disappointment or

Maybe …just maybe, fulfillment.

The mommy, I recall those productive years.

She is at her peak, and I look at her knowingly,

Nodding at her gratefully, for the job she has.

The fifty something who still has the spark, my vision is still clear,

Her appeal has not dimmed, as she approaches the ridge to the other side.

The grandma, my eyes embrace her, capturing the total woman, who awaits her time.

November 2015

CIGAR CHARACTERS

Cigar stores and lounges are a meeting place for a subculture of smokers, complete with a collection of the greatest guys and damaged wackos imaginable.

Men from eighteen to ninety sit around in leather and faux leather chairs, watching Wheel of Fortune in the morning, Fox News, sports of all kinds, or sometimes just an old movie.

Smoking anything brings many disease possibilities to the human body. Every smoker knows this from the endless advertisements and smoking bans around the country. Cigar smokers are generally in denial about the health risks, but an oral gratification fixation may be a common psychological trait among them.

Every lounge has their share of eccentric characters. Here are just a few that are among the most memorable:

Take "Sauce guy," the smoker who puts hot sauce on his cigars. Tabasco Sauce is amateur status. Mid-sixties, short with male pattern baldness, sauce guy wears a tracksuit that went out in the seventies. He uses Mexican hot sauces, jalapeno, habanero, Scotch Bonnet, or ghost peppers and other unpronounceable sauces that can take the paint off cars. "The hotter the better," he spews, his eyes teary while puckering his cheeks as he sucks in wind to reduce the sting. Sometimes he never even lights up. Often, when he uses the men's room, the moans were like someone being tortured during the Spanish Inquisition.

Then there's "The Spitter." He stares at the other smokers waiting for someone to say hello so he can snub them. Five foot ten with a scraggly beard and a zippered, blue jacket, the spitter looks like Charlie Manson a week before he died. His favorite contact sport is bullfighting. I kid you not. This guy smokes his stogies down so low that he burns his fingers, all the while spewing up spit and phlegm into a plastic bag. Not just a polite little spit, mind you. The Spitter makes a noise like your grandfather made when he first woke up in the morning. He brings it up from his testicles, globbing a green ooze that looked like the slime Regan projected in the Exorcist.

How about "The Billionaire?" Late sixties, a head of hair like St. Anthony of Padua, this sick bastard had fellow smokers convinced that he was a Wharton School graduate and had the biggest house in Las Vegas. He even had photographs to prove it. You know, those real estate photos from Lifestyles of the Rich and Famous. Mind you, he wore clothes that I wouldn't wear to paint my living room, smelled like ass, and stole five cigars a day which he stole from the humidor. From the worn, fake leather, maroon Havana chair at a famous lounge, The Billionaire made amazing deals from his cell phone… deals worth tens of millions of dollars, with letters of credit flying around the country in his wake. He sold every posted commodity, from crude oil to sugar to diamonds. He proclaimed one day in a booming voice, "There is a global sugar shortage. I have the sugar, fifty metric tons a week, and Coca-Cola has to buy from me. They have nowhere else to go." He has bigger balls than Andrew Carnegie and lies better than Hillary Clinton. Well, maybe not better, but at least as much.

"The Bigot," who hates everyone. Late fifties, tall, blue eyes, with an air of an Aryan master race tank commander from World War II. He curses the Jews and Blacks of course, because they are the reason Obama ruined the country. Fox News is his bible and the leggy ladies on the set makes him moan in ecstasy.

"Uber Dave," mid-fortyish, blue jeans, and work boots, Dave looks like his belt buckle is ready to explode from just one more beer. Dave drives around picking up fares from his cell phone. He proudly tells everyone how he could bang every female passenger that enters his car, describing the ladies in explicit detail. Every sentence he says must have the word motherfucker included.

"Buffalo Bob"…five feet five, built like a fireplug, poor thing suffers from severe OCD, reputedly washing his hands in the men's room until they bleed. Then shakes everyone's hand in the lounge, proud that he recalls everyone's name, "Lou, right…yeah, Lou, that's your name…see? I remembered…Lou…Louie!"

"The Talker." A mountain of a man. Has to be six foot seven with a George Harrison haircut wearing a camouflage jacket and shorts. The Talker talks to no one but himself...and he gets answers. Voted most likely to come into the lounge with an automatic weapon killing six guys as they puff away.

"Butt Guy" goes into the red bucket where the staff throws the used cigar butts. He looks like a cross between Jimmy Fallon and Louis C. K. He grabs every smoked cigar butt he can, putting them into a plastic bag. Then he smokes them. He thinks anything over a half-inch is a windfall.

"The Rich Guy." Six feet and fifty pounds overweight, mid-fifties, with jet-black hair that looks like a bad hairpiece. "I have eight, eighty-inch, flat screen televisions in my house. I need them to fill up the ten thousand square feet," He brags. "Just traded in my Rolls for a Bentley. Got tired of the Rolls after three years," he intimated. I only smoke Cubans...the sticks you smoke are pure shit," he bellows. "My wife, she spends fifteen thousand a month on herself. I hope she keeps under twenty a month. My girlfriend is already in double figures."Without a doubt, Rich Guy has a two-and-a-half-inch penis.

"The cop"...twenty-eight. Handsome as fuck, he collects as many phone numbers as he can from the other smokers and then sends group porn texts. Not just regular porn, which wouldn't be the worst thing that happened. He sends amputee porn, midget porn, that sort of stuff.

"Bag man" is five-foot-five, grey hair, with a Julius Caesar haircut. "The Bag" wears a colostomy bag and smokes the cheapest cigars available. He says that he no longer needs the bag but uses it for convenience. The guys think he's too lazy to wipe his own ass.

"John," the self-proclaimed, self-hating Jew. Tall, middle-aged, bald guy with two diamonds in each ear. Super smart photographic memory type, especially when it comes to Nazi history and movie stars. Big John was pushing four hundred pounds until he had the gastric bypass operation. Now he looks almost human as he keeps a keen eye out for any female who happens to walk into the store.

Then he's off to the races with every filthy comment that has ever been imagined.

"Joe, the lawyer." Brilliant guy with lounge hours from 9:30 in the morning until 3:45 in the afternoon. Comes with a bag of way too small black tee shirts. He changes shirts before he goes home to his wife. Joe looks like a full-back which he was in high school. The lawyer sues people all day from his cell phone that he views over the rim of his reading glasses. Class action suits are his game, cigars are his life. Every tee shirt is peppered with small burn holes which he wears as badges of the trade.

"The Pedophile"... Nicest man you ever met. Bookish computer geek who sat for hours and hours with his laptop and cigars. Giving computer advice to whoever asked. That is until someone recognized him. The cop ran his rap sheet and found fifty-one arrests from child porn to molesting underage kids from Thailand to Canada. He was summarily chased from the lounge, laptop, cigars, and all. He's awaiting sentencing.

I guess I fall into the category of weird cigar smoker as well. The writer who brings his laptop, memorializing the characters who he sees several times a week.

PAROCHIAL

Fifty years after I graduated from Catholic high school in the Bronx, New York, I am still lamenting about the experience. Actually, I want to partially air my continued anxiety on the totality of twelve years of parochial education.

It took me ten years after my mother's passing to be able to write something, knowing the sacrifices she and my dad made to pay for the schools. Money was always elusive to my family, so the tuition and the demands from the church for further donations were a big burden. My feelings toward the parochial education and the church itself border between guilt and ungratefulness.

The options where I lived were not good. It was either Catholic school, full of religion, strict educational demands, and discipline, or the public schools that offered none of the same."I would rather be beaten by the brothers and nuns than beat up or stabbed by the white trash, blacks, and Puerto Ricans who were in public school," my best friend recently said to me. We had all those types in the Catholic schools but they were, as I was, from good families trying to escape the yoke of prejudice.

Put aside that I started elementary school at the too-young-age of five years old, with no kindergarten, directly into the brutal hands of the nuns who did not spare the rod. On my first day of first grade, I was smacked because I would not comply with the sister's command to hold a little girls hand while in line. I was not an especially compliant child, and the good sisters were not about to put up with any of that. They broke me quickly like a palomino who refused a rider.

The Irish kids were the majority, as were the nuns and later on, in high school, the Christian Brothers. These kids had already been exposed to the faith by their quasi-religious parents. It also seemed that these kids all had a nun or priest somewhere in their family. That gave additional, instant credibility to the nuns and priests. The extent of religion in my immigrant, Italian family were statues, medals, and superstition, like burying a statue of Saint Joseph upside down in the yard to sell the house quickly.

The stories of the birth, death, and resurrection of Jesus were all nice enough and somewhat entertaining. To me, those events mostly meant days off from school, Christmas gifts, food, guilt, new clothes, and more food. To the Irish kids, it seemed like they were devoted to believing what they were being told. For me, by third grade, I had already rejected all the nice stories and categorized them into the same myth as Santa Claus, the Tooth Fairy, and the Easter Bunny. My lack of compliance was evident if only to me, but I have a sense that my boredom was duly noticed as rebellious.

My academic record was poor. Maybe worse than poor if I'm being totally honest. I always felt inferior to the Irish kids who seemed to be favored by the nuns, brothers, and priests. Was it that I didn't care enough, had a creative mind, or just could not grasp arithmetic and math? Or those silly diagraming a sentence with the noun, verb, adverb and predicate lines. Or did my feeling of not being as smart as the other students define my twelve years under the crucified Christ we were told to adore?

A "C" was an acceptable mark for me. My parents had no choice but to accept my grades, not knowing how to help me improve. Or perhaps it was what they were being told by my teachers. "He does not apply himself." I had been categorized as a failure at a young age and accepted that moniker until I got into college, where incidentally, the Irish Christian Brother high school guidance counselor told me not to apply. Senior year, the good brother told me to take the Sanitation Department test or work with my uncle making pizzas. That's what Italians should do anyway,

From the first slap for not complying to the ultimate slap to define me as a worker-bee, my worth in the eyes of those who made the rules was as an underachiever. Maybe I was. But I always felt these religious people were all basically prejudiced or got their comfort in life from hiding behind a robe and a wooden cross.

I always viewed the church as a place for weak people to band together and feel better about themselves. Not really a bad thing when you think about it, but I still, in my mind's eye, see the way those nuns, brothers, and priests viewed me. I was one of the great unwasheds, a peasant who didn't fully buy into their well-crafted stories.

Now don't get me wrong. In spite of my lack of religious fervor and my negative frame of reference toward the church, I don't want to go on a one-man crusade against one of the largest groups of believers in the world. I truly feel they don't need any help in minimizing their value as a respectable organization.

Someone said that what the Arab world is doing today is actually a reverse crusade. I must say that along with the wonderful stories and myths that were taught to me, the Crusades were among the best-spun stories of them all. We were taught that the crusaders were sent to spread the word of Jesus to non-believers. In essence, to save their souls from eternal damnation. I had a picture in my mind of these fabulously outfitted soldiers with that magnificent red cross down the front of their uniforms, riding into foreign lands on splendid white steeds with the Roman Catholic Catechism in their gloved hands. I had imagined those soldiers of Christ sitting down with the non-Catholics and answering what we as Catholics knew to be absolute fact. The fifth line in the catechism is: "From whom do we learn to know, love, and serve God?

"We learn to know, love, and serve God from Jesus Christ, the Son of God, who teaches us through the Catholic Church." Essentially, the Crusades were saying, *forget the whole Muhammad thing and the Quran, because our myth is much better than yours.*

Research shows, however, the Crusaders had no Catechisms. They only had swords and other weapons of war. If you didn't go for their story and wanted to believe in some other fairy tale, the price was high.

For those who did not comply, they received the ultimate slap. They lost their lives, their families were devastated, their tents were scattered, and their wealth taken.

The ancestors of the doubters, who tasted the cold steel in the name of The Christ, imparted in them a very long memory.

Sixty-two years after my first experiences with the church, my feelings have not softened toward their many fantastical stories. In fact, my feelings toward how they said I should have lived my life is meaningless. The feelings of fear and guilt that was drummed in never sat well with me. In fact, I couldn't care less about their damnations, their story of everlasting life, their never-ending need for money, and above all, the arrogance which proclaims their way is the right way. The only way!

The physical, emotional, and spiritual abuse that was done behind the weapon called Jesus Christ has continued for centuries. In my reality, it ended with me.

The smack I was given on the first day of school is a microcosm of what I witnessed over twelve years. An anxiety-based education that I would have been happy to have done without.

RIKERS STORY

"I got thirty years of stories. None of them good," Marc said.

Rikers Island is a jail operated by the New York City Department of Correction. Rikers is not a prison but a jail, mainly housing detainees that are remanded to custody and await conviction or have short sentences. The jail is located on the East River between the boroughs of Queens and the Bronx. There are over twenty thousand detainees on Rikers Island. The maximum number of prisoners is fifteen thousand.

The Tombs, officially called the Manhattan Detention Complex are two fifteen story towers, located in lower Manhattan which houses only male inmates, mostly pretrial detainees. The jail is designed for nine hundred and twenty-five inmates. It houses over three thousand.

Marc is a new acquaintance from one of my cigar haunts.

Marc and two of his buddies, Vinnie and Freddy, all three recent retirees from the New York City Correctional System, sat in brown, Havana chairs, puffing on cigars…and drinking Hennessy Cognac. They were drinking more than puffing.

"If any corrections officer tells you they don't drink they just plain lying," Marc said. Marc's voice was sharp and clear, his accent pure Bronx and his cadence on the edge of jailhouse.

Vinnie and Freddy agreed just like those men behind a Baptist minister, testifying to Marc's righteousness.

"Nothin' good happens in that place. Just nothin'," Freddy adds.

"Can you tell me a few stories about Rikers?" I ask.

"We worked the Tombs, too," Vinnie chimed in, "and that shit is worse than Rikers, if you can believe that," he adds.

"We all retired, but we still drink. This is the only thing that keeps you in balance, this here booze," Vinnie instructed as he held up his glass.

"Ok, we got a story for you. Vinnie, tell him about shit-man," Marc orders.

They all cringe and let out a guttural moan as I looked from guy to guy wondering what the hell they were about to tell me. I relit my cigar and sat back ready to take every bit of this adventure in.

"This inmate one day, ok, he wasn't in for no heavy charges. Just some normal stuff like possession or something like that... I don't remember exactly what, but it was no big deal. So, he come out of the cell, now mind you there is just me and my partner," Vinnie begins.

"How many inmates in the unit?" I interrupt.

"Fifty inmates per guard, and that's just fuckin' wrong," Marc answers.

Vinnie continues.

"So, this inmate just rips off his clothes and goes into the middle of the cell block, butt-ass naked. Just naked! And he takes a shit right there in front of everyone while he screamin' about some bullshit. Then he just takes the shit and starts smearing it all over his body. On his arms, neck, his legs, his face, all the fuck over his self."

"Look here…you know how the Indians put on their war paint? He took his shit...his literal shit, man, you follow me? And put it here and here with two fingers." Marc used his fingers to show how the prisoner had painted his face on his cheeks under both eyes.

"Then what?" I ask sitting upright in my chair while the smoke swirled around me.

"Then what? I call the Deputy Warden. He tells me what to do officially," Vinnie said.

“So, I guess there's an official and unofficial version?” I query.

“Damn straight. I’m gonna tell you the official version. Still bizarre as fuck. Ok, we were ordered to get the rookie officers, dressed from head to toe in hazmat outfits. Three officers, goggles, gloves, the whole nine. They were ordered to subdue the inmate and clean him up and get him into solitary,” Marc adds.

“Unofficial version?”

“Six officers surround this dude with fire extinguishers and hose the motherfucker down like he a beast. Then we kicked his ass in,” Vinnie bellows.

“And then, and then...then we go to his cell, motherfucker, and he already smeared more shit all over the place. On the doors, the door handle, the walls…it was baaaad,” Marc added.

“What I can’t understand is how a guy can just shit on command like that. He just kept shitting and pulling it out his ass. Nasty!” Vinnie blurted.

By now I am practically rolling on the floor laughing and I signal the long-legged waitress to come over because I already know I'm going to buy these guys a drink.

“Have you guys ever seen any high-profile people?” I manage to get out between laughs.

Marc jumped on my question. “All the time. I processed Madoff, Gotti Junior, Robert Chambers...”

“Yeah, Chambers. He choked that girl out in Central Park. Good lookin' dude, that Chambers,” Vinnie interrupted.

“I remember, I remember," I said, "and Gotti Junior? What happens when those mob guys get brought in?” I asked.

“No one bothers with them. Everyone can tell who they are. Nobody fucks with 'em. The inmates know they have to go back on the streets one day. Mob guys have the streets,” Mark stated.

“What about child molesters and rapists? I always hear they are treated like shit in jail,” I asked.

Freddy jumped in on that question. “Luckily for them, no one knows right away what they are in for until they get arraigned. Then they go into court with other inmates. The inmates hear what the charges are and, well, that information is brought back to the cell block. After that? They're fucked; they get abused every day after that. Every single day. It’s really bad on those dudes; I sure as fuck wouldn't want to be one of them. Guys built like Mike Tyson mess them up good.”

“Good," I said, "So, what group does have it easy inside?"

“Gang members. There's lots and lots of gang activity. Once the Crips and Bloods give their hand signals, those guys are protected. Same with M-13 gang members. But guess what group has it the absolute best?” Marc asked me.

“No clue,” I responded.

“Orthodox Jews."

The waitress came by with the drinks and I stopped her as she was setting down the drinks and I said, "Maybe you'd better cut this guy off. His stories are getting more outrageous." We all laughed except the poor waitress who had no idea what we were talking about.

"Once they call the Rabbi down, he axes them a few questions to see if they really be Jews, then the Rabbi calls upstairs and gets the judge to do a fast arraignment, and they are out. They have amazing power within the system. Better food, too,” Marc stated,

"Get the fuck outta here," I responded. But all three guys were adamant.

Vinnie took a long pull on his Hennessey and changed the subject. “One day, I think it was the same day as shit-man did his thing, there was this woman officer who got in the middle of an argument with two inmates. She was about to get her ass kicked good, so I step in. I shoulda have minded my own business and let her get smacked up.”

"So, what happened?" I queried.

"I step in to break up the beef and...you know that metal piece on the bottom of a mop? That long-ass, steel bar? So, the inmates take it and use it as a weapon. This dude comes from behind me and whack. He opens the back of my head wif the metal piece. I had all to do not to pass out and go down. He would have finished me off for sure," Vinnie lamented.

"Christ, almighty. Have any of the officers ever been killed?" I asked.

"No, but one of our officers had his head bashed in by a dumb-bell. We had brought in some weights so these dogs could work out. The prisoner kept hitting one of our guys with the dumbbell until we jumped in to save him. It left him totally crippled," Marc answered.

"And after, I had my head opened, too, and I got two days off. No compensation for ninety stitches in my head. They suck!" Vinnie added.

"You boys are open season. How do you guys not let this affect your home lives, you know, your personal lives?" I ask.

"Booze, brother. This shit takes the edge off," Mark answered.

NOIE AND OLYMPIA

In 1949, in the town of Castellammare del Golfo, on the island of Sicily, Olympia Russo's family was making the long-awaited wedding plans for her. According to tradition, Olympia's train from her veil would be twenty meters long, a meter, which by custom, is for every year of the couple's engagement.

And this was going to be no ordinary wedding, mind you. The Russos were compare, dearest friends of the Abate family for as long as any of the town folk could remember. The two families' friendship went back generations, as did their partnership in the fishing boats which sustained both families' livelihoods.

Olympia Russo and the son of the family, Noie Abate, were born just days apart in 1929, brought into this world by the same midwife who had attended their own mothers. Olympia and Noie were both birthed in the same, fluffy, homemade feather bed while their fathers were attending to fishing nets and boats, each one secretly hoping for a boy to be born to eventually help take over the duties for supporting the household. Olympia would have been Olympio, but God had other plans.

Olympia and Noie, through their parents, were promised to each other from birth; it was a promise neither family would disavow.

The year Noie and Olympia were born, the Great Depression in America had placed itself, like a blanket of poverty, over the entire globe. The Russos and the Abates, two families who knew how to stretch one lire into two, shared the same, small, stone house just like many Castellammarese had done during those years. Long before the collapse of Wall Street in New York City, and in turn, the world-wide economy, poverty was a condition of life on the northwest coast of Sicily. The thing about these two families is that they had no idea they were poor. They had everything they needed and more important, everything they wanted.

Why? Because the patroness of this once Arabic-controlled town, Santa Maria del Soccorso, Saint Mary of the Rescue, to whom many prayed to seek her intercession with Jesus, provided everything the fisherman required to sustain their lives and bring children into the world as soldiers of Christ.

The legend of their patroness goes back to a battle in the harbor of Castellammare del Golfo between Spain and Savoy, Italy in 1718. The fight was for the possession of all of Sicily.

A Spanish ship had taken refuge in the harbor of Castellammare after being pursued by five British warships. That old, Arab castle, yes, the Arabs controlled Sicily for two hundred and sixty years, until they were thrown out in 1091 after being ruled by thirteen Muslim Emirs, was where the Spaniards took refuge.

The town was being pummeled from the warships as the townspeople prayed for a merciful intervention. Suddenly, as the cannonball's fire lit up the night sky, a Madonna dressed in all white, along with a row of angels, appeared, scaring the British fleet shitless. The limeys fled, and the town was saved.

Just four years later, however, it was said Santa Maria del Soccorso needed another angel, so she took Noie's father in a sudden and ferocious storm while he was out on one of the boats fishing for tuna. Noie, being only four years old, and his mother already having five other children, was sent to New York City in America, to live with his father's brother for a short while. That 'short while' lasted until Noie was twenty.

Meanwhile, Olympia grew into a red-haired, blue-eyed goddess who they said took after the Normans who came into Sicily after the Arabs. I will not digress.

All her life, Olympia had a photograph of the four-year-old version of Noie among her sacred rosary beads and prayer cards. She had no recollection of Noie and, other than an occasional letter from the uncle in New York, there were no accompanying photographs of her future husband.

Olympia was being taught by her mother, aunts, and Noie's mother to be a good wife for Noie. She was taught to cook, sew, fix things, care for children, and worship Santa Maria del Soccorso. All the while, every red-blooded, Sicilian fisherman in Castellammare del Golfo had it for Olympia. So much so that her mother began rumors that she was promised to a famous hometown boy who ran the American mafia at that time. Each suitor was given a different story to make them keep silent or perish. Mobster names like Sebastiano DiGaetano, Salvatore Maranzano, Stefano Magaddino, Vito Bonventre, John Tartamella, and Joseph Bonanno were all evoked by the treacherous Signora Russo to protect Olympia's honor for her compare's son, Noie. Those men were embroiled in what was called the Castellammarese War in New York at the time. Everyone was killing each other to be top dog. The last thing they were thinking about was some greenhorn, redhead back home.

Noie had really just finished high school at Theodore Roosevelt in the Bronx, NY and was now an apprentice plasterer with his uncle and cousins. He was a bit too young for World War II, but he had flat feet and a heart murmur which would have kept him out of the military anyway.

Noie loved being with his cousins every day joking about the beautiful girl he was to marry back in Sicily. The cousins made fun of Noie, though, who took it in stride, because Noie had big ears, an oversized nose, and was sure to lose his hair before he was twenty-five. Other than that, Noie was, like his mom and dad, short in stature but big of heart. Noie would, as they say, give you the shirt off his back.

Truth be told, Noie's uncle hadn't sent a photo of his nephew for fear Olympia would take the first fishing boat or train to Palermo.

Virtually the entire population of Castellammare del Golfo, the Sea Fortress of the Gulf, waited with great anticipation for the upcoming arrival of Noie Abate.

In a few months, on August 19th, the town would hold the annual pageant of Santa Maria del Soccorso with all the religious fervor that went along with it. Noie would be arriving on the first day of the feast.

Noie flew from Idlewild Airport in New York to Rome and then on to Palermo where he took the train to small Castellammare. No easy trip in those days.

Noie alighted the train carrying two bags. One with his clothing and one with gifts for his intended bride, her family, and his very own dear mother.

A small group of locals, with their beloved instruments, serenaded, and were there to greet Noie, along with his mother, cousins, old friends, and curious neighbors.

Olympia and her parents were standing next to Signora Abate and her other children, who were all dressed in their Sunday best clothing.

Several young fishermen, all rejected suitors of Olympia, with the traditional fishermen hats and blue scarves tied around their tanned necks, were also on hand to see their competition. Seeing Olympia in her special, green dress, which was made for this occasion by her aunts, was an added benefit to the men who knew they could only dream of being with her. The young men puffed on Marlboro cigarettes in the red pack, their only exposure to American culture. They sat on fruit boxes away from the family and friends of Noie Abate.

The band struck up a tinny sounding Sicilian song as Signora Abate ran to her long-departed son. Long hugs and kisses and a reintroduction to Noie's siblings had many in the crowd wiping away tears of joy.

The band played on as the young fishermen strained their necks to see the lucky American. They looked at Noie and then at each other with stunned amazement. This was who would be marrying the most gorgeous young woman in all of Castellammare? This dopey-looking, big-nosed runt with elephant ears and a receding hairline? Murmurs and snickers were heard throughout the crowd.

One of them said he must indeed be part of the New York Mafiosi and have money longer than train smoke.

At last, Noie hugged and kissed Signora and Signori Russo, who were both crying like babies, remembering the day Noie's father was taken by the sea and Noie had to leave for America.

The crowd parted, and Noie and Olympia were standing face-to-face for the first time in sixteen years. Noie had remembered his bride-to-be had flaming red hair, and Olympia only knew a photo of a dark, four-year-old boy in baggy, homemade clothes.

Noie was literally stunned at the sheer beauty of Olympia. He was intimidated, looking down at his shoes for what seemed forever. Olympia's fair skin blushed almost as her red as her hair. She looked at her mother for guidance. Her face said this man is the one you promised me to? This is who my husband will be?

Noie did not look up at Olympia or anyone else for that matter. He quickly fumbled through the bag that carried the gifts, fishing out a wrapped present for his intended wife. Noie handed the package to Olympia, his eyes still downcast, his face betraying his awkwardness.

Olympia looked at her mother who smiled through her tears and was clasping her hands. Signora Russo nodded toward the package, giving her daughter her approval to open the gift. The crowd looked on in great anticipation wondering what amazing gift the American would bestow upon this lovely girl.

Olympia fumbled with the wrapping, her mother holding it so the gift would not fall to the ground. When the last of the paper was pulled away, Olympia's face glowed with a smile as no one had ever seen.

Noie had hand carved a plaster statue of Santa Maria del Soccorso for his new bride-to-be. He hand painted the Madonna's flowing red gown that covered her feet. Around her shoulders was a light blue coverlet that also covered the saint's head. Atop the Holy Mother's head laid a brown and gold crown. Our Lady of Rescue held out a black wooden stick in her right hand. In her left hand, she held the hand of a young child, all in white, who stood at her feet gazing up in wonder at the Madonna.

The crowd gasped in approval. Signora Abate covered her mouth with both hands, and the tears fell from her eyes like a fountain. Many in the crowd clapped, and a few knelt as if to say a brief prayer.

The young fishermen were stunned at the simplicity of the gift. After all, shouldn't a rich American present a woman as lovely as Olympia with expensive gold jewelry or maybe even a car? One of the boys smacked one of his friends in the back of the head before he dropped a just lit cigarette to the ground twisting it under his boot.

The simple, yet thoughtful gift expressed Noie's devotion to the patron saint of Castellammare del Golfo.

Noie would make a perfect husband, Olympia thought.

The band led the procession of people around the Cala Marina, past a small, sandy beach where the crowd dissipated, and everyone walked up the ancient walkways to their homes. Olympia walked with her parents and siblings. Noie walked with his own long-lost family.

The Russo and Abate women prepared a sumptuous fish and homemade macaroni dinner in honor of Noie's return. Olympia made a cassata dessert from her great-grandmother's recipe that had everyone fawning over her with delight. The women discussed the wedding plans late into the night. Signori Russo, his sons, and Noie's brothers got acquainted with Noie over bottles of red wine and charcoal-roasted chestnuts after dinner.

The feast and festival of Santa Maria del Soccorso was officially the first date for Noie and Olympia. By tradition, Olympia was never really near Noie and never out of sight of Signora Russo and her sisters and her compare Signora Abate. There was a least a five-foot distance between the two fidansante at all times. Holding hands or walking arm-in-arm was just not done in public, and certainly, there was no private contact allowed.

The festival was a special event with dozens of colorful, Sicilian, horse-drawn carts that came from as far away as Palermo to win a prize for the most elaborate design. Scenes of Sicilian country life were painted in bright colors onto the carts, some as old as one-hundred years, passed on for generations. Some of the horses wore towers of ornate flowers and feathers atop their heads and backs. Red, pink, and yellow pom-pons adorned the carts and horse. Noie and Olympia selected their favorites. Sugar cubes were fed to the horses by the couple's younger cousins who would take the treats from Olympia's handbag.

On both sides of the Cala Marina, booths were set up for the feast. Dried candy, fresh fruits with white grapes the size of golf balls, trinkets, balloons, toys, paper birds on thin sticks, and street food were enjoyed by the residents and visitors to Castellammare. Ceramics vendors laid out their wares on the ground hoping for a few sales during the three-day feast.

Olympia would catch Noie staring at her, wondering why he looked dazed as if in a daydream. Noie noticed Olympia was the focus of attention of the men walking along the Cala. Old and young, married or infirmed, all noticed the statuesque and stunning young woman with the blazing, red hair. Noie was both proud and jealous. He had no frame of reference to deal with his feelings.

With August being torrid in Sicily, a cool breeze from the gulf was a welcome respite for Noie who was not used to the sub-tropical heat of his homeland. His dark blue shirt was stained with perspiration, yet Olympia looked as fresh and sweet as a slice of local melon.

The couple knelt as the statue of Santa Maria del Soccorso passed them; the Madonna, the patroness, was carried on a special cart manned by the elders of the church. Monsignor Monteleone, who would officiate at the wedding of the sweethearts, stopped and blessed the couple. Noie kept blessing himself like a victim of St. Vida's Dance. His awkwardness was noticed by the young fishermen who mimicked his rapid signing. This was noticed by Olympia's father and uncle who had a word with the young men. Whatever was said, the young men disappeared into the crowd, not to be seen again.

Over the next three months as the wedding day approached, the only other 'dates' Noie and Olympia had were the after dinner passeggiata, the walks around the town, attended by a phalanx of women who always accompanied them. At no time did the couple touch, from the time Noie arrived at the train station, until after they were married.

The wedding was plain, simple, and religious with a morning high mass said by the Monsignor. Noie and Olympia, now man and wife in the eyes of God, walked through the town, she in her grandmother's white wedding gown, and he in a black suit with the traditional bola tie of Sicily. The young fishermen were nowhere to be seen that day.

The outdoor meal complete, the wedding guests dissipated into the town until just the immediate family remained.

Now, the first problem of Noie and Olympia's marriage reared its head. It was now only mid-afternoon with the blazing, Sicilian sun relentlessly beating down on Castellammare.

What was the couple to do? It was still daylight and consummating their marriage at that time of day was an issue. How could they have their wedding night during daytime?

It was decided by the mothers, the couple should go to the cinema and see a movie before going to their wedding bed in Olympia's aunt's house. Her widowed aunt would, in turn, stay with Olympia's mother for a few days as planned so the newly wedded couple would have their privacy.

Noie, Olympia, and Olympia's cousin, Paulo, who would act as the couple's driver for the day, went to see a double feature in the town's small movie theatre.

Riso Amaro, Bitter Rice, starring Silvana Mangano, Doris Dowling, and Vittorio Gassman was followed by the raucous comedy starring Gino Cervi and Gina Lollobrigida in La Sposa non può Attendare… The Bride Can't Wait.

Noie and Olympia could barely focus on either film, both in anticipation of the coming consummation. However, Paulo who fell asleep during Riso Amaro, roared with laughter at the Lollobrigida comedy.

All the while, Paulo sat between the newlyweds.

Paulo drove the now shaking couple to the aunt's house. Noie sat up front. Upon arriving, Paulo offered them buona fortuna as they exited the tiny Fiat.

Once inside the quaint but small, stone and plaster home, the couple shared a chilled prosecco, which was left on the kitchen table along with two glasses. After most of the bottle was drunk, the couple made their way to the bedroom. Well, at least Noie did. Olympia made a beeline for the tiny bathroom. She locked the door using the small, metal, hasp hook lock.

Noie undressed to his underwear and hopped under the home-crocheted comforter, awaiting his bride.

He was more than ready for Olympia.

She, however, would not come out of the bathroom.

Her mother, new mother-in-law, and aunts prepared Olympia in many ways: Cooking, cleaning, darning, ironing, and sewing, but she had absolutely no idea about making love. Noie waited as patiently as he could for nearly an hour.

Finally, Noie got fully dressed again and tried to cajole Olympia to join him in bed. He spoke through the door in as gentle a voice as he could muster. She wouldn't budge from the room though, nor would she unlock the door.

Totally frustrated by his new bride, the rejected groom left the house and walked down the street to his mother-in-law's home. Noie explained his plight as Signora Russo bit her hand.

Signora Russo and her sister walked arm-in-arm to see Olympia and explain things to her. Noie was commanded to remain outside the small house until he was summoned. He paced and prayed to Our Lady of Rescue for guidance and patience.

Suffice it to say, the advice given to Olympia by her mother and widowed aunt would not be needed in present-day society. Olympia was told, after her weeping subsided, that she needed to do what she had to do for the marriage to go forward and not embarrass herself and the entire family. Her mother told her to just close her eyes and let Noie do the work. Her aunt assured her it would not take very long and maybe one day she would possibly even enjoy it. Together the three women prayed to Our Lady of Rescue for Noie to be patient and quick.

After a few months, Noie decided that he was not suited to be a fisherman in Sicily for the rest of his life. He contacted his uncle back in New York who assured Noie his job as an apprentice plasterer was secure, so the young Mr. and Mrs. Abate settled in Yonkers, New York.

The statue of the Madonna, presented to Olympia from Noie at the train station at Castellammare del Golfo, still stands upon the buffet table in the Abate dining room sixty-nine years later.

With four children and six grandchildren, Noie and Olympia share their devotion to Santa Maria del Soccorso with their now growing family, passing down the feasts and traditions which go along with it and retelling the story of how they met. This special feast day is also still celebrated by the Abate family back in Sicily as well.

A new tradition is started with the grandchildren who put beautiful, fragrant, fresh flowers, carefully arranged in a vase behind the hand-carved statue twice weekly.

BEFORE I DROP DEAD

"C'mon Jimmy. That's not very nice," Julio replied.

Jimmy Cataldo, sat alone at a table for six, in his brother-in-law's restaurant on Arthur Avenue in the Bronx. He peered up at Julio, his reading glasses perched on the bridge of his ample nose. 'Jimmy Snaz' ran the books for the Lucchese family.

"Not very nice, but very true. Every Puerto Rican I ever met was a thief or a liar. You come in here with some bullshit why you don't have the vig for me. You were due yesterday. HowlongIgottawait? Before I drop dead? Where's my fucking money, you Spic fuck?" Jimmy seethed. He rubbed his thick hands together like he was about to get off his chair and smack the thirty-year old Julio.

"I tried to explain that my wife got sick and my son, too. She didn't go to work for a week and the kid needs…"

"I give a fuck! The deal was made very clear. You bet on the Giants and you lost. You couldn't come up with the grand so I lent you the cash. The points are ten a week. In my world that's a hundred a week. You now two weeks late so the points are twenty. You owe me three hundred plus the thousand. What don't you understand about this, you retard?"

"That game was a lock, Jimmy."

"That's why they call it gambling, fucko. If they got that field goal you woulda been in here the next day to collect your winnings. Now you come up with some Rican lie about your wife and kid. Go get my three hundred," Jimmy bellowed. He leaned his three-hundred pound, five-foot-six frame back in his chair.

"It's no lie, dude. She's really sick. I had to take off work today to take her to Barnabas. I dropped the kid off at child care, and they wouldn't take him because he's sick, too. I had to get a babysitter before I took my wife to the hospital. They say it's pneumonia and she had to stay. No lie," Julio said. He was almost in tears.

"First off, I'm not your dude. Second, I don't give two shits about your problems. Now go get my three hun, you lying, Puerto Rican prick."

"Jimmy, why do you hate so much? You take my action for the last two years. I've never been late before. What does my being Puerto Rican have to do with this?"

"You people came here when? In the late fifties? You ruined my neighborhood from back then. Burned down half the Bronx and robbed what was left. Took welfare from the city since the fifties."

"I was born here, Jimmy. I went to school with your son Vincent, for Christ sake," Julio implored.

"Fuck that shit. There was a time that your kind and the niggers couldn't even walk through this neighborhood to get to Fordham Road, without getting your heads split open. Tell your story walkin,'" Jimmy muttered.

"I wasn't even born then! I'm not like that and you know it. I have a good job. My father and mom never took a cent from welfare and neither have I and I never will. I just got balled up and I need some time," Julio spouted. The young man was showing anger in his dark eyes.

"Time is money. Pay for the time but be on time with your vig. And watch your tone with me, spicko. You see those two guys over there at the bar? I snap my fingers and you will be in the bed next to your pretty wife at Barnabas."

"That's not nice, Jimmy. I apologize if my tone was a bit off, but all you've done is insult me since I walked in here."

"You insult *me* by not paying. Now how would it be if I let every slimy spic who walks in here not pay me? There has to be respect for me and mine. So before I drop dead, go borrow the money and come back and pay what you owe. You got till tonight or expect a visit. Case closed. Now get your slimy ass out of this joint."

Jimmy Snaz lifted his girth out of his chair with a threatening move toward Julio. The two beefy thugs flew off the barstools and went over to the table.

"Problem over here, Jimmy?"

"Nah, this guy is just leaving," Jimmy laughed.

One of the tough guys opened the restaurant door while the other pointed to the exit.

Jimmy Snaz' day continued much like any other. Bets were placed, money was collected. The numbers runners came around with their slips. Jimmy ate a huge lunch of veal parmigiana with a big bowl of spaghetti and meatballs, half a loaf of seeded Italian bread, a bottle of wine, and two, homemade cannoli, washed down with three cups of espresso corrected with anisette.

Julio went to Barnabas Hospital to visit his wife, checked on his son, and went to work. His worry gave him acid reflux to kill a horse.

The two thugs made their rounds terrorizing the locals who owed vig to Jimmy and returned in time for a seven o'clock dinner with their boss.

The restaurant started to get crowded with the evening diners. Jimmy's cousin pointed to tables as the busboys placed baskets of bread, small dishes of olive oil, and plates of cheese and salami on the tables of the new, hungry patrons. The waiters hustled with the drink orders, and back and forth into the bustling kitchen.

At seven, Jimmy and the two thugs placed their dinner orders after a few Cutty Sark scotches, still at the same table where the Snaz held court all day.

As the restaurant dimmed its lights for the evening guests, Jimmy's mood also darkened.

"Youse guys may have to pay that young spic a visit tonight. He lives in that building on Belmont where Lefty's mother used to live… rest in peace," Jimmy whispered as he blessed himself in memory of his friend Lefty's late mother.

Suddenly, and without notice, Jimmy Snaz put his beefy hand on his chest.

"Jesus Christ, this agita is bad tonight," Jimmy proclaimed. He suffered from chronic heartburn, no surprise after what he consumed at lunch.

Jimmy's eyes rolled back into his head. His barrel chest and thick head fell onto the table, spilling his glass of scotch and a bottle of Pellegrino water.

"Holy Christ, Jimmy...Jimmy, you okay?"

Jimmy's cousin ran to the house phone at the bar. He dialed 9-1-1.

The two thugs moved Jimmy onto the floor, tossing his chair aside like a rag doll. Jimmy was as blue as a summer sky.

The screaming siren of an ambulance, weaving its way up Arthur Avenue could be heard in the distance. Jimmy's color was now a purple hue.

Six minutes after the call, a F.D.N.Y. Emergency Unit pulled up in front of the restaurant.

Julio walked into the place, in his paramedic uniform, complete with a cardiac resuscitation unit in his hand. The driver, a black guy, and his black assistant followed into the restaurant with the wheeled gurney.

Julio spotted Jimmy on the floor along the two helpless thugs standing over the prone gangster.

The young first responder went to work immediately. Jimmy's pulse was weak and he wasn't breathing. His color betrayed his cardiac infarction.

Julio cleared the overweight man's airway and started cardiac-pulmonary resuscitation. The Snaz' color began to return a bit but there was still no solid heartbeat.

Julio quickly decided to use the paddles on Jimmy to shock his heart back to a normal rhythm.

Once, twice, three times before Jimmy's overtaxed heart responded.

Twenty-four minutes later, after the two black attendants took the Snaz a block away to Barnabas Hospital Emergency Room, Jimmy was admitted to the cardiac care unit. Julio was next to his patient every step of the way.

The doctors stabilized their patient and Jimmy was admitted to the Intensive Care Unit. Julio's ambulance was called to a stabbing on Southern Boulevard, six blocks from the hospital.

At eleven the next morning, Julio went to visit his ailing wife. The attending doctor informed the young man his wife was improving but more tests were needed. She would likely remain at Barnabas for four or five days. She was young and strong and would be fine the doctor said to Julio's great relief.

Not knowing Jimmy's condition, or if he even survived the heart attack, Julio made his way to the ICU.

Jimmy survived and was sitting up in his bed, tubes streaming from his arms, mouth, and nose, the two thugs standing guard on either side of the bed. Flowers were already sent by the mob clan and left with Jimmy, despite hospital policy.

Julio cautiously entered the gangster's room.

"Ohhh. Look who's here. It's the hero kid," Jimmy whispered through his tubes.

"Hi, Jimmy. Glad to see you made it," Julio said.

"I heard what you did for me. My guys here were amazed how you saved my life."

"It's my job, Jimmy," Julio uttered.

"After how I treated you, you could have let me croak right there on the floor."

"Never!"

"Well…thank you, Julio. We're even now."

"Nah, Jimmy, I'll pay what I owe. That's how I roll," Julio announced.

"Bullshit! Now don't insult me, please."

Jimmy looked at one of the thugs and pointed to Julio. The hefty thug handed a white envelope to Julio with a wide, gleaming smile.

Jimmy swallowed hard and tried to lift his girth to sit up…to no avail.

"There's three K in there for your kid only under two conditions: You accept my apology for the shit I said to you, and, if I hear about you gambling again, I will get out of this bed and kick your ass myself."

Julio was nonplussed. Tears filled his eyes. "Thanks Jimmy. Thanks!"

ELROY PEANUT BUTTER

Savant syndrome is a condition in which someone with significant mental disabilities demonstrates certain abilities far in excess of average. The skills at which savants excel are generally related to memory. This may include rapid calculation, artistic ability, map making, or musical ability. [Usually just one special skill is present. It is estimated that there are less than a hundred savants with extraordinary skills currently.]- Wikipedia

I was doing research on autism and came across this definition of Savant Syndrome.

It struck me that there are very few of these specially gifted people in the world.

I was also amazed by the fact that I actually knew a savant when I was a teenager. Problem was, when we called him retarded, in spite of our amazement at his particular skill, Elroy went nuts.

His name was Elroy. We never really knew his last name but we did know that he lived in one of the eight story attached buildings on Rosedale Avenue in the James Monroe housing projects in the South-East Bronx. Just recently, friends who knew him better than my crowd said his last name was Steele. I can attest that he was as strong as any steel made.

Elroy was more than six feet tall. It was difficult to tell his age but we knew that he was older than us because of his need to shave. Like many black men, Elroy had a good many razor bumps on his face and neck. These ingrown hairs caused Elroy to scratch at them often, making the condition worsen.

If he asked for a sip of your soda, you took a big guzzle and gave Elroy the rest of the bottle for fear of catching whatever he had. His nose was always dripping and the drool ran from his mouth constantly.

For whatever reason, he picked up the nickname Elroy 'Peanut Butter' which he enjoyed when he was called that name. However, and it's another urban mystery, if you said to him, "Elroy Peanut Butter, your mother sweats malted milk," he would attack you with vicious man-strength, and your ass would be kicked. How and where this malted milk "sound-out" occurred we may never know. He was once seen taking out three older guys who tried to rob a group of his younger, white friends. One of the three called him nigger and that was all she wrote. Elroy took them apart with ferocious intent. Yet, when a young friend of his, Arnold Wolf died of a brain tumor, Elroy was devastated and not at all embarrassed to display his tears.

Elroy had a lower lip that seemed to run down almost passed his chin, exposing his pearl white and perfectly shaped teeth. His gums and inside lip were a reddish pink which resembled an evening fall sky. Elroy's head was always tilted to his right side and his arms seemed longer than they should be. His coke bottle-like thick, horn-rimmed eye glasses were always falling down off the bridge of Elroy's nose. He constantly pushed the glasses back up his nose with his middle finger. All of the nails on Elroy's fingers were bitten down almost to their cuticles in what looked to be a painful undertaking as he chomped away.

Elroy Peanut Butter's long-left arm was always up by his left ear, a small transistor radio pressed closely to his ear. Elroy would sing along with the music of the day, not missing a single lyric or note.

However, singing the music and knowing all the words, was not Elroy's given talent.

The young man could recall any record label, in perfect detail, of any 45-rpm vinyl record, ever produced. He even knew the flip side, usually an obscure recording just to get the main song published.

A few of our crowd would test him from time to time when there was a lull in the action. We weren't teasing him at all. He was utterly amazing in his detail and depth of memory.

"Hey, Elroy Peanut Butter, what's happnin'?" One of us would yell out as Elroy walked by. He would walk over and sit on a parked car with us, or on a park bench, depending where we were. He never made eye contact with any of us. It seemed like Elroy was either looking up at the sky or down at his well-worn sneakers as he spoke about the 45s.

If Elroy was walking in the projects with his mama, we made no contact with him whatsoever. She had an incredible meanness about her. Perhaps severe is a better description of the woman. Elroy's mama had a certain look that could scare a dog off a meat truck. Elroy always walked five steps behind her, his eyes concentrating on the ground ahead of him, his transistor radio tucked away in one of his pockets, his usually smiling face scowled into a look of anger.

On one particular summer day, it was actually too hot for us to be playing one of our many ball games. Elroy was walking by and we invited him to come under the cool shade of the double building's breezeway.

"Okay, Elroy, here goes!" someone would say.

"*Dancing in the Street*," someone else would lay down the challenge.

Elroy lowered his transistor radio and then relayed all of the information on the record label as if he were reading it from the inside of his thick glasses.

"*Dancing in the Street*, Gordy Records. Martha and the Vandellas, written by Stevenson-Gaye, a product of Motown Record Corp. Produced by Wm. Stevenson Time 2:37 45RPM. 1964 Copyright Motown Record Corp, Jobet BMI."

"And the flip-side?"

"Flip-side to *Dancing in the Streets* will be, *There He Is*, produced by Holland Dozier…"

"Okay, Peanut Butter, we got it!"

One of the girls in the group asked, "Elroy, can you name some of the other songs Martha and the Vandellas did?"

"There was *Honey Child, Quicksand, Heat Wave, Jimmy Mack...*"

"What's the flip to Jimmy Mack, Elroy," Someone else blurted,

"*Third Finger, Left Hand.*"

"Let's try another. One of my favorites, '*Walking in the Rain,*" another gal asked.

"*Walking in the Rain,* Philles Records, The Ronettes, written by R. Spector, B. Mann, C. Weil, Screen Gems Music, BMI, Time 2:38, Arranged Jack Specs Nitsche, Engineer Larry Levine ,123. Flip side, *How Does It Feel?*, Philles Records…"

"Okay, Elroy, that's enough… man you are great!" the girl interrupted.

"Yeah, but he only knows the colored music," a skeptic announced.

"No, sir, I know all music," Elroy corrected. He looked up at the sky and smiled.

"Okay, let's try the Beatles!" one of the guys yelled out.

"*I Want to Hold Your Hand,*" the same girl challenged.

Elroy smiled with a look of confidence that he enjoyed with nothing else in life. He couldn't even tie his shoes or dress himself.

"*I Want to Hold Your Hand,* Lennon-McCartney, Capitol Records, Duchess Music Corporation, BMI 2:24, 5112, 45X 4471, Recorded in England, Manufactured by Capitol Records Inc. USA TradeMark Capitol Records Corp."

"Flip side?" the skeptic yelled.

"*I saw Her Standing There,* Lennon-McCartney…"

"Man, you are boss!" the skeptic interrupted Elroy and became a believer.

This would go on and on as we sat around Elroy Peanut Butter wondering how he did this?

"I can't recite the ten commandments and this retard can remember every shit on every 45 ever made. I don't get it," one of the guys announced.

Elroy didn't seem to hear or be at all bothered by the insult. He put his transistor to his ear, smiled, and waved good-bye.

When I drive through the neighborhood, over fifty years later I wonder about a lot of the guys and girls I grew up with. Vic the cop, Johnny Boy Toronto, Ski Jump, Joey Dark Glasses, Sis, and Angela… and Elroy Peanut Butter.

What kind of life did he lead? Is he alive? What happened to him if his mama passed? Where did he end up? Did anyone ever get away telling him his mother sweat malted milk?

ELIZABETH DOWD

The young Catholic priest stood beside the bed of the dying old woman.

Elizabeth Dowd was not at all religious, but she checked a box that said Catholic when she entered hospice care at Calvary Hospital three weeks ago. Elizabeth was baptized eighty-two years ago by her strict Catholic parents. The last time she entered a church, though, Pope Pius XII was the Supreme Pontiff.

"Ms. Dowd? Ms. Dowd, can you hear me?" the priest asked.

"Yes, I can. I'm not gone just yet," Lizzy replied. Her eyes remained closed. The last time anyone called her Lizzy was more than thirty years ago. It was at her mother's wake. She hadn't seen nor heard from any family member since.

"Ms. Dowd, I can hear your confession now. Then serve you communion and administer the Sacrament of the Anointing of the Sick."

"Thank you, young man but I have already made my peace with God. I've never really believed in any of it but I did ask for forgiveness just in case." A quiet chuckle left Lizzy's lips. Lizzy was all but ninety-pounds, her skin drawn tightly around her skull, her eyes deep set with large, black circles around them. Her breathing was labored and her chest heaved with a gasp when she inhaled.

"That is very good, Ms. Dowd. I see by your chart you have no family and that you have made final arrangements for yourself. Can I be of any comfort to you at this time? Perhaps we can say a prayer together?"

The priest wore a white vestment which hung past his knees. Over the garment, draped over his ample shoulders, was a purple stole with gold piping, and a red and gold embroidered cross on both hanging sides.

"Feel free to say and do whatever you care to. My time is very short and I don't wish to be insulting with my last breaths. I had plenty of practice doing that in my life." Lizzy pulled in a deep breath. Racked with cancer, she was in no pain but on the verge of losing consciousness. The morphine saw to that.

"I will anoint you with this oil and holy water and forgive you your sins Ms. Dowd," the priest uttered. He was used to seeing people near death but rarely were they as alone and as distant as Lizzy Dowd. He tried on a number of occasions over the past weeks to comfort her and pray with her. At least this time she was civil.

The priest blessed the dying woman, and dimmed the lights to the room half way. Lizzy Dowd would die quietly and alone.

Not long after the priest's visit Lizzy went unconscious for the last time. She knew life was slipping away from her but that didn't faze her nor worry her in the least. Lizzy had enough. Enough of life, enough of the doctors, nurses, and certainly enough with this cancer which ravaged her once robust frame.

Lizzy drew her last breath alone but with comfort and dignity.

A tingling in her face and scalp, like needles and pins by the hundreds, and bright light everywhere was her next experience. The light was so bright she even tried to open her eyes to look around, but the light's intensity forced her to keep them closed. The fragrant aroma of honeysuckle and lilacs waffled over her.

I told them no services, no flowers, no box, just bring me somewhere to be burned up, Lizzy thought.

The light dissipated and Lizzy's eyes fluttered open. She was amazed at how clearly she could see. Those annoying floaters in her eyes were gone as was the hazy tunnel she seemed to have the last few years. Lizzy felt her body was featherlike, her movements effortless. No ache in her abdomen where the cancer started, her hands were straight again, and there was no pain in her hip, no pain anywhere for that matter.

Lizzy looked up to a magnificent blue sky with billowy white clouds that seemed to be placed in perfect order. She found herself sitting under a willow tree with a noiseless, babbling brook just below her feet, the soft sound of chirping birds in the perfectly formed trees all around her. Beyond the brook a green and yellow colored glade framed the lush bushes and trees on hills that seemed expertly painted. A warm breeze rustled the foliage proving the vegetation was real.

Heaven? Can't be! I always thought that was a fairy tale like everything else that spewed out of their mouths. This is just my mind showing me something nice for the last time. Then, vast nothingness. Peaceful, non-existence, Lizzy thought. She inhaled the sweet-scented air, filling her lungs to a capacity she recalled as a young woman. No cough followed, no sour taste from medicine or blood.

Okay, let's get the hell out of here; that's enough. Let's admit I'm dead and move on.

Lizzy rubbed her eyes half-hoping she would not disturb the messages from her subconscious which were sent to comfort her. She realized what she was experiencing was real.

No longer and old lady, Lizzy bolted to her feet and stood tall, her back straight as when she took ballet classes a million years ago. She let out an audible sigh.

Now if a guy dressed all in white with a puffy white beard comes around, I'll have some explaining to do.

Wait! Is that laughing? It sounds like kids laughing. Now maybe I'll find out where the hell I am. Oops…wrong choice of words, Elizabeth, Lizzy thought and admonished herself.

Lizzy walked a bit, following the sounds of talking and laughter. She walked along the brook until she came to a wooden, arched bridge. The scene reminded her of a Monet painting she once saw in a museum.

The sound of children talking became clearer. It sounded to her like little girls at play. Lizzy calmly made her way over the bridge, her feet seemingly gliding rather than stepping.

On the other side, Lizzy saw two young girls sitting together on a plain, teak wood bench playing with porcelain dolls. The dolls were dressed identically like the girls, in knee length dresses. One girl and her doll in white, the other girl and doll in lavender. The girls, nor the dolls, wore shoes.

"Ahh, pardon me…where are we?" Lizzy blurted.

The girls giggled into their hands.

"Some people call it heaven. We call it home," the girl in lavender said.

"You just arrived, I guess. We can show you around if you want. My name is Mattie, and this is Becky. Who are you?" the girl in white added.

"Well, my name is Elizabeth. But you can call me Lizzy. I think I just died and came here somehow."

"You are so pretty. Here, come join us for a while," Mattie offered.

Lizzy joined the girls on the bench. Becky offered her doll and a small hairbrush to Lizzy who began to slowly stroke the doll's blonde hair.

"It's been a very long time since I played with dolls. This is so nice," Lizzy announced.

"We are a lot older than we look, but we both decided we wanted to remain little girls for a while. We are sisters, you know!" Mattie blurted.

"We can be any age we want to be," Becky added.

"Well, how old are you?" Lizzy asked.

"If we were alive I would be fifty-seven and my sister would be fifty-five," Mattie replied. Becky shook her head in agreement. Both girls wore their blonde hair in ponytails.

“We were tiny babies when we got here,” Becky added.

“How do you know that?” Lizzy queried.

“We know lots of stuff. Tell us about you. How was your life?” Mattie asked Lizzy.

“It was long. Long and lonely, I might add,” Lizzy lamented.

“Did you have a husband? Any children? Do you think your parents are here? Do you want to find them? We can show you how,” Becky proposed.

Lizzy let out a laugh. "You both are so adorable! Okay, I would love for you to show me around."

The three walked hand in hand, one little girl to Lizzy's left, the other to her right. They talked and laughed and had the most splendid time together walking around heaven.

"No husband, no kids." Lizzy answered their questions as they went on. "I came close to marrying once, but it never happened, and the time just never seemed right for me to have children."

Finally, they came to a rest and sat down, the two girls leaning their heads against the newcomer, Lizzy.

"That walk was so wonderful!" Becky exclaimed.

"It sure was!" Mattie chimed in.

Lizzy replied, "I'm so happy to have met you both!" as she wrapped one arm around each girl cuddled next to her and kissed them both on the top of their heads."Do you have any other questions you wanted to ask of me?"

"Yes," the two little girls said, as they looked up adoringly at Lizzy, tears streaming down their cheeks. "Why did you abort us?'

GASPARE MICELI

Gaspare Miceli, my grandfather was born in Sicily in 1888. He came to the United States in 1891 with his mama and two siblings.

Known as Papa to his five children, and Aspanu to his Sicilian mother, later in life his kids would call him the Sheik of Fordham because of his handsome, dark complexion and his philandering with the ladies. One of his daughters, my mother, Mildred, was the last family member to have a talk with him a day or two before he passed on at the age of 72 in 1961 when I was ten years old.

Three wives and a few girlfriends along the way, Jasper as he was called in English, was the kind of guy who would call my mom from Florida, or Niagara Falls, or the Catskills for a few bucks to be wired so he could return home after one of his assignations. His first wife died of the Spanish influenza in 1917 leaving him two children, Uncle Pete and Aunt Dora. He met my Nanni Lena at the Roseland Ballroom and she became his second wife. Nanni had passed away five years prior to Jasper. He quickly married a younger woman, Rose, and he figured out soon enough, that he couldn't live with her. He moved in with his daughter, my Auntie Eleanor and her family in the Bronx. Jasper and Lena also had Uncle Anthony to round out the five kids.

Jasper's last conversation with Millie was seemingly a premonition of his death. It was early on a Friday evening.

"Ya know, Millie…I'm not gonna live forever. You reach an age when it's enough," Jasper lamented.

"Oh, Papa you are in great shape for your age. You will live to be a hundred," Millie offered.

"Sure, I will. Just listen to me. When I die I want Rose to get my plumbers union pension. She is still legally my wife and she's a nice lady. Mama is gone so why should the pension go to waste? Ya hear me?"

"Of course, Papa. Rose is nice... it was just her rotten kids you didn't care for."

"What kids? They are all married. They treated her like dirt and I couldn't watch it anymore. At any rate, see that she gets the money… you promise?"

"I promise."

"Other than that, I don't have much so I'm leaving you kids with nothing. I'm sorry about that," Jaspers voice trembled.

"First of all, you're not going anywhere for a long time and second you lived your life. You don't owe us anything so stop that kind of talk.

"Okay, Millie, just do what I ask, would ya please?"

"Papa, are you feeling alright?"Millie asked.

"Not myself lately. A lot of aches and pains."

"So, cut back on work. Plumbing is a young man's job. Come over Sunday for sauce. I'll invite everyone."

"Maybe next week. I have plans for the weekend."

On Monday afternoon Millie got a call from her brother Pete.

"Millie, it's Pete. The old man dropped dead. They found him under a sink in Queens. He sent the helper down for a tool and when the kid came back he was gone."

"Are you sure? I just spoke with him on Friday. This can't be!" Millie cried. She could not wrap her head around the situation.

"I'll be sure when I see his body. Is Joey home? I need him to come with me to claim the body in Queens."

Off my dad went with Uncle Pete to identify Papa's body and make the arrangement.

Millie called the other siblings giving them the bad news and no one could believe this virile, healthy man was gone. Aunt Dora said he told her he was going to Miami with a Jewish woman he met at the Young Israel of Tremont dance on Clinton Avenue and 180th Street. How could he have died in Queens?

Auntie Eleanor said he wasn't home for a couple of nights. The Sheik pitched his tent in a lot of places.

Uncle Anthony was sullen and went right for the sunglasses.

Uncle Pete and my father identified the body at the morgue and signed some papers to release the body to the Walter B. Cooke Funeral Home on Jerome Avenue in the Bronx, near Fordham Road.

My dad said he looked peaceful but he didn't like that his hands were still tied in a string and he told the clerk so at the coroner's office. That was the extent of the viewing. Uncle Pete was too upset to talk to anyone about it.

The next night, as was the family tradition, everyone gathered at Cooke's and waited for the eldest kids, Pete and Dora to get to the viewing room before the undertaker opened the green plastic louvre doors to see Papa. His name was affixed to a small metal plate above the door. Gaspare Miceli.

Most of the family didn't even know that was his birth name but there it was, he was an official dead person.

At 6:30 P.M. everyone arrived and the louvre doors slid open as expected.

The five kids were the first to enter, the women in all black dresses and veils, Papa's two sons in dark sunglasses to prevent people from seeing their anguish I suppose.

"Pete, that's not Papa. Look…it's not him. I told you he is in Miami with that Jewish lady," Dora screamed. She fainted dead away caught by her husband before she bashed her head in.

In the casket was not the Sheik of Fordham, the salt and pepper haired, dark Sicilian heart throb of the neighborhood. Rather, a man in Papa's suit holding his rosary beads seemed a cross between Jimmy Cagney and Richard Harris. Irish as Paddy's pig with white hair and a bulbous nose that saw a few too many boilermakers in his time.

"Millie…Millie…that's not Papa…I knew it…I knew he couldn't be dead," Eleanor howled before she crumbled into a black sack in front of the casket.

Pete and Anthony just looked at each other in disbelief as Millie walked up to the Irishman.

"Well, they sometimes change when they die. It could be Papa I guess."

"Millie are you drunk? I seen him…It was Papa. Joey was right there with me. It was him…DEAD!"

The undertaker interrupted the opera. "Is there a problem?"

"Yeah, there's a problem alright. See this face? My face? That's the face that should be in this box lookin' up at us. That ain't my father, pal," Uncle Pete seethed.

In the meantime, Jasper's grandkids were celebrating that Papa wasn't dead but in Miami with a Jewish lady. Some of the younger ones started to run around the metal gray folding chairs exclaiming, "Papa's in Miami, Papa's in Miami."

The celebration of life was short lived.

"Does he have any identifying marks on his body, Mr. Miceli?" the Cooke guy asked.

"He has a tattoo of the crucifix on his arm," Uncle Anthony murmured. He began moving into the undertaker's personal space.

"Which arm?"

"Which arm? He only has two arms, you idiot. Look at both of them. I'm telling you this ain't my father," Peter hollered.

They used smelling salts on Dora. She kept coming to and fading back.

Eleanor, now up from her faint, called Pete and Joey morons for identifying an Irishman.

The kids and cousins were all chased from the room and the louvre doors were closed while the undertaker removed the dead man's jacket to see his arms and the tattoo of Jesus on the cross.

Muffled talk. Some louder muffled talk and the crash of those metal chairs and we all knew that the undertaker was knocked into next Tuesday by one of both of Papa's sons.

When the police left it was determined that the man's name was Patrick McGinnity. Papa was at Thomas M. Quinn & Sons Funeral home on Broadway in Astoria, Queens.

Uncle Pete any my father hailed a Yellow Taxi on Fordham Road and sped to Quinn's.

Joey walked in first, all five foot-six inches and one hundred and ten pounds of him, followed by Pete whose hand was throbbing from its meeting with the Cooke guy's jawbone.

Sure enough, there was the Sheik of Fordham in a poorly fitted suit and a silly grin the undertaker plastered on his face.

The McGinnity family was standing around showing pictures and passing around a couple or three flasks of Four Roses rye whisky.

"Ah, excuse me! Jesus Christ Almighty. This is not your guy…this is our guy. What the hell is wrong with youse people," Joey bellowed.

A couple of Irish giants staggered over to the sawed-off guinea.

"What a ya talking about for fook sake? They told us ole Patty just got a bit dark from the death, is all."

Joey and Pete tipped a few with the McGinnity's and the arrangements were repaired.

Years later I went with my mom and dad and Uncle Pete to Saint Raymond Cemetery to visit Nanni and Papa's grave.

Uncle Pete knew where the site was, as he was a regular. He took off his hat and addressed the grey granite stone.

"Hi, Mama…look who I brought….Millie. Mill, I don't think the old man is home today. He may be in Miami with that Jewish lady."

THE FRONT ROW

I remember clearly
Being in the sixth row.
Paying little, if any attention, to the
Box in the middle.
Ignoring the words spoken from the lectern.
Knowing there was sadness in the five rows ahead.
Unconcerned. Death was so far away.
When in the fifth row,
Able to see the lectern a bit better
But still, not paying much attention
Seeing the shaking of the gray hair in the first row,
So far away, only glancing at the closed rectangle.
Forgetting now, how I thought about being in the
Fourth and third rows.
Dammit, I was much too busy to think about the box.
Let's just get this thing done and continue.
In the second row, not long ago,
Looking at the slower moving ones in the first row.
Sitting alongside the box now, feeling it a bit closer,
Still unconcerned, listening to a few choice words
From the lectern. Seeing how those in the first row
Were reacting in somber words, in controlled silence.
In the first row now.

I look back beyond two, three, and four.

Paying attention only to the sixth row.

I smile at their lack of fear, poking away at one another.

Almost laughing, both them and me… and reprimanding eyes.

From the third and fourth row.

My attention turns to the box.

I remember who lies inside, fondly sometimes.

Other times, sadly, and others, with nothing on my mind.

Still without fear, without worry, for when I

Am in the middle.

Again…not paying much attention to the lectern.

They are only words still.

TWO WISHES

Walking on the beach at Montauk Point at the very end of Long Island always makes my mind wander. On this particular overcast fall afternoon, I tried to relax from the pressures of everyday life and simply enjoy the moment. Problem is…I can't do that.

I'm that person who has a difficult time becoming part of the gray sky and the crashing waves that send a mist of cold water onto my face, leaving liquid dots on my blue wool pullover. As lovely as that sounds, I sometimes get annoyed by the ocean showing off all its power.

Waves pummeling the sand and rocking the beach in an explosive force often startles me, reminding me of being bombed from an unseen enemy.

The birds flying over the ocean, squalling, wailing, chirping, cawing gets annoying after awhile. I look out onto the vastness and tumult of blue-green water and see a fishing boat rocking back and forth, rising high above the tide and my stomach does a backflip.

Then, from out of nowhere, I think about Balsamic versus red wine vinegar. A large hermit crab in the wet sand suddenly brings me back to nature and I begin breathing in the crisp ocean air again trying to clear my thoughts and become one with nature.

The aroma reminds me of Vincent's clam bar and my mind goes to the hell-fire hot sauce they serve on the fried calamari.

Jesus Christ…can't I just at least try to learn to relax and go with what nature is offering here? I think to myself.

I try to avoid that beige and white sea foam or the salt water from getting onto and into my new blue and gray running shoes.

I need running shoes like I need skies. I barely want to take more than a two block walk. A hundred and thirty nine dollars. I'm an idiot, I lament to myself.

Okay, that's it...I'm going to Zen myself into enjoying this beach and this water and that pukey fishing boat if it kills me!

I close my eyes and for a minute, maybe ninety seconds, my mind goes blank, and I am totally relaxed and become one with nature.

My mind goes off again. *Could that Montauk Conspiracy thing be real? After all, this place does have that kind of creepy, mysterious feel to it. That whole Camp Hero, Montauk Air Force station thing where the government and the CIA had an underground base where they were working on psychological warfare, mind control, time travel, alien life contact, and teleportation. Who knows? Stranger shit has happened. Richie and his son Justin believe it all to be true. Maybe they dropped too much acid, who knows?*

And the ghosts at Montauk Manor...that's a whole other story. But this CIA-Air Force conspiracy theory goes back a while. Just like that crazy Montauk Monster that washed up over here. A mammal with a bird's beak and a dog's jaw. Shit gets crazy here...probably from all the sun and drinking.

I walked awhile longer along the beach, the clouds darkened, the air smelled now of rain and salted fish. My mind raced to the many conspiracy theories that abound. *The Kennedy Assassination, how aliens helped the ancient Egyptians build the Pyramids, General Patton's death, Roosevelt knew of the bombing of Pearl Harbor...the Natalie Wood death... Marilyn Monroe murder or suicide, the Black Dahlia...*my head was spinning.

So much for a relaxing walk on the beach. I need to up the meds or start drinking like everyone else.

Near the black slate-like boulders that surround Montauk Point there are also great slabs of concrete that were left on the shoreline after World War II.

That's when the Navy did torpedo testing on Navy Road...lots of history here...town is from 1660. Who knows...George Washington's congress commissioned this lighthouse...

I glanced up behind me at the over one-hundred foot white and maroon painted sandstone lighthouse…

Imagine that! George Washington? I wonder what this place was like in the seventeen nineties? I thought…my mind visualizing horse drawn work wagons and men with beards and women in long dresses with big sagging breasts.

Then I saw it!

On the beach, near the twisted concrete bunker like slabs and stone boulders that protected the tip of Montauk from the unrelenting ocean, I saw something sticking out of the sand. Rusted orange, it looked like the closest thing to an Aladdin's lamp that I'd ever seen. It had a long-curled handle, some of which had eroded away from exposure to the elements, I imagined. The front of the lamp had a stumped spout that was encrusted with small barnacles, around what looked to be an opening at one time. Its top seemed to be removable except for the seal of rust around the circumference. The bottom was caked with barnacles, some larger than the crustaceans seen on the spout.

My luck…the guy who found this before me is dating Kate Upton and won the seventh game of the World series and has fifty million in cash, I thought. Then I laughed out loud.

I rubbed the lamp with my right hand, feeling pieces of its surface rust scraping off and onto the sand.

Oh well, a decent burial I suppose.

I used the heel of my running shoe to start a hole in the sand and wound up using my hands to go down about a foot into the dry, pebbly sand. I dropped the lamp into the hole, my mind a blank, and covered the lamp with sand. I patted down my work with both running shoes and started walking again toward the very point of Long Island.

"Pardon me, sir." A voice came from behind that gave me a momentary startle. A young man stood there wearing a small turban and a large white smile. His teeth seemed too white perhaps because of his dark olive complexion. He was a bit portly and wore a close-cropped beard. His clothes would be considered robes like the Hari Krishna wear. I judged him to be in his early thirties.

"Hello…you startled me. Where did you come from?" I asked.

"Well, sir…I came from the lamp you just buried."

"Ha ha ha…Yeah, sure pal. Okay, where are the cameras? Real nice try, kiddo," I blurted.

"Not kiddo…my name Dawad Kassis. I am genie of lamp. I bid you peace."

"This is a funny prank. Did that fucking Richie Zurrow put you up to this, kid?"

"I have your language but don't understand some of words. Fucking, kiddo, kid, prank…"

"I mean, it's a joke young man. I get it. You will now grant me three wishes and I will be a billionaire and jet off with three Victoria Secret models."

"Sir…there is no secret. Also, I not young man. I have over six hundred years and I will grant you just two wishes, sir."

"Where did you learn English David. You don't mind if I call you David, do you?"

"David is fine sir. I had six hundred years of study many language. English is difficult…yes?"

"You're doing pretty good David. You need some work on prepositions and plurals but you're good to go."

"What may I call you, sir?" Dawad asked.

"You may call my friend Richie and tell him he's a funny man. Okay, I'll play along…you can call me Lou."

"Very well, Lou. Now to business. This is last time coming from lamp for me. The first two did not end well because of greed. Now I am freed to live a normal life without powers."

"So, how many wishes do I get, Dave?"

"Just two, Lou. Just two so choose wisely. You may not wish for material items. No wealth, no women, no property. Only…I can take you back in time to see two things. Any two things you desire. From dawn of mankind until yesterday. I will transport you back in time so you can be a witness of history. We will return upon your desire."

"Dave, I'm really afraid of heights so forget that magic carpet ride thing. I can't go in an MRI and I can't do high…oh and I can't swim. Food? I have no problems, none at all," I laughed.

"Lou, my new friend. There is no carpet. I will the time and place and we are there," Dawad said. His teeth gleamed and his large brown eyes sparkled.

"I still don't believe a word of what you are saying, Davey, but give me a minute to think about what I want to see, will you?"

"Lou, after our trips, I am free. I have waited long. I can wait more to begin a real life."

"I have a good deal on a condo in Boca…only kidding, Dave. Just let me think."

I pondered for a few minutes, my brain going like a computer. First, I thought of the Montauk theory, screw that…then Kennedy… who cares we know it was the mob anyway. Stonehenge…no interest. I got it!

"David, I'm all set. I have the two places that I would like to go."

"Very good, my friend, Lou. A few rules, please. You cannot talk or touch any people, so you cannot change history. When you wish to return, we come back here in a flash," David explained.

"Got it!"

"Tell me where you wish to go at this time, please."

"Both places or just one?"

"Both please my friend, Lou."

"Okay, here goes. My first place would be to see the resurrection of Jesus Christ. The moment that he came from inside the tomb three days after he was crucified and was once again alive. I want to see that with my own eyes because I've never really believed in that kind of thing. You know the whole faith thing. If I could see it, then I would believe it."

"So why not the birth of Jesus then?" Dawad asked.

"Dave, listen to me. It's the resurrection that's the big thing in Christianity. If he doesn't rise then there is no religion…period. Then it means the billions upon billions of believers who, for two thousand years believed, were duped, defrauded, and taken for a ride. Who cares when or where Jesus was born? Let's go back to the big event. The first Easter Sunday. No bunny rabbits, just the son of God rising from the dead. Maybe then I can believe and pass the word on."

"It seems you have struggled with your faith, my friend, Lou." Dawad's smile was bigger and brighter than before.

"Nope. Never struggled a day with it, Davey. Just never had it inside me to believe any of this nice story."

"And your second wish?"

"Okay, here goes. What would I have been without my parents?" I asked the genie.

"Well, perhaps adopted?" Dawad responded with a question.

"No…no I mean if they never met. Never created me?"

"Nothing my friend, Lou. You would be nothing."

"Correct, my friend, Dave. That's why I want to see the moment my parents met. The first time they saw one another. Can you do that, Davey?"

"I still think this a bullshit deal and a joke but let's see what ole Dawad bin Laden pulls out of his turban."

"Lou, my friend. Come, stand next to me. Where we are going is very cold but I will keep you warm. Not to worry. Please close your eyes and count backwards from ten.

With a smirk, I followed Davey's instructions. I took a deep breath of the Montauk ocean air through my nose and heard the kwah of an overhead seagull. I got to two and I knew my surroundings had changed. I was in a snowstorm.

"Holy shit, Dawad. Holy shit. It's a blizzard. We are in a blizzard!"

"Yes, Lou. This is where your parents met. It is December 26th, 1947. We are in New York City. Borough of Bronx. There will be over sixty-seven centimeters of snow in two days," Dawad proclaimed.

"Feet, Dave…what is that in feet?" I asked rather than try to recall a formula.

"Oh, about twenty-six feet. This snow was called a mesoscale blizzard. The snow fell only in a small area. It covered New York City entirely," Dawad explained.

The genie continued."Look, see that young woman coming? The one who is fighting against the wind. That is mother."

I couldn't make out her face. The woman was covered from head to toe. Black snow boots, a gray cloth coat with big black buttons, a white homemade knitted hat with a gray pom-pon atop. Her face was covered from the wind and falling snow with a red and black scarf, and gray mittens finished off her emergency snow suit. She held her arms close to her body as she fought against the strong wind and pulverizing snow.

"Lou, look across the street. Can you see? That young man about to come to this side. That is father."

"That's my dad? Holy crap…that's him. I've seen photos of him in that coat. How young and skinny! My God!"

Joey was trying to cross the street never thinking about looking for an oncoming car, bus, or truck. The city was paralyzed from the blizzard. He wore black snow boots, brown corduroy pants, a blue pea coat, its collar turned up, a scarf around his neck, brown gloves and a fedora pulled down so as not to blow off of his head.

"Little does he know, when he crosses Tremont Avenue he will meet the love of his life. The mother of his three sons. The woman who would be with him until the cancer got him," I said aloud. The tears started to roll down from my eyes. I did nothing to stop them from dropping onto my tee-shirt. That's when I realized I was standing in a blizzard and not at all cold as Dawad promised.

"Watch closely now, my friend, Lou. Wait for moment they meet. It arrives."

The young woman, head down, walked toward the corner of the street. Four feet of snow was piled up on either side of an icy walkway. The wind nearly took her aloft as she hunkered down making herself smaller.

At the very moment Joey and the young woman were within five feet of each other, the lady slipped and fell into a snowbank. She made a muffled thud into the snow and started laughing at the scene.

"My God, are you, all right?" Joey asked. He bent down on one knee to see if he could help somehow. The lady was hysterical laughing.

"Sure, I'm fine."

"Here let me help you to your feet," Joey offered.

The young lady got on her feet with Joey's help and they both slipped momentarily but didn't fall. She began laughing again, holding on tightly to Joey's arms.

She brushed the snow from her coat and hat and took the scarf down from her face to straighten it.

Joey was smitten.

Her face was like a porcelain doll. The blush she had on and red lipstick she wore was mostly worn away from the storm but she needed no makeup. She wore glasses, as did he. Her eyes were the size of the large, black olives his mother put out for the holidays. Her smile illuminated Joey's world.

His entire face had a few pimples and was all lit up like yesterday's Christmas tree. His full head of wavy black hair was exposed and he tipped his hat to the lady. She noticed he had a nice smile. He was speechless.

"Thanks, so much. It's very nice for you to offer your help," she said.

"It's very nice of you to fall…I mean…It's nice to meet you. I'm Joey."

"I'm Millie. Thanks again," she said as she started to be on her way.

"WAIT! Can I walk you home? You know, just in case you fall again, I mean."

"Sure, I live just two blocks from here on A-hun-eighty-first Street. That's nice of you to offer," Millie said.

"I'm on Clinton and A-hun-eightieth. We're right around the corner from one another. Here put your arm in mine in case you slip again. I'll make sure you don't fall."

Millie and Joey walked down the snow and ice covered concrete pavement toward 181st Street. They would have me in 1950, a year after they married.

I stopped, standing next to Dawad the genie, watching my parents go into their future, together holding onto each other until Joey died at age fifty-eight. Millie never married again.

I got down on one knee, the snow not bothering me a bit and cried into my hands. I saw Millie and Joey meet for the first time. How many people even know when or where their parents met? I got to see it.

"Lou, my friend. Are you ready to return to beach?" Dawad asked. He was still smiling with a hint of moisture in his eyes.

"Yes, my friend, David. You are an amazing man."

"Okay, please to stand next to me, close eyes, and count back from ten again."

At the count of seven I could smell the ocean again. Time did not seem to pass in Montauk, but I could feel a few raindrops starting to fall. The seagulls flew quickly looking for their nests and some cover.

"That was the most amazing experience of my life. There they were, my parents, in living color, in a snowstorm. I cannot thank you enough. My God, they were so young and vibrant and…and young! Did I say young? He was so handsome and she was drop dead gorgeous."

"Yes. They were a handsome couple, Lou." Dawad uttered.

"I'll never get over this moment in time. Now, on to see the resurrection of Jesus Christ," I shouted.

Dawad looked down at his sandals, seemingly inspecting the sand between his toes.

"Davey? Davey, what's up? Let's go see Jesus. The tomb where they buried him. What is that? Jerusalem?" I blurted like a kid in a carnival.

"Lou. My now dear friend. I hope you find your faith somehow," Dawad stuttered.

"What do you mean? You said two wishes. I asked for two, I saw one. What is this, a discounted deal? C'mon, I'm dying to see the resurrection."

"I can do many things, but this wish I cannot do. Whatever you have left in your life, I hope you will be happy," Dawad said. His glowing smile was gone. His features became dark and he looked as if he were going to cry.

Dawad turned and walked down the beach, his elegant robes flowed inland from the ocean. He covered his turbaned head from the rain with a white wrap-around garment.

I stood there in stunned silence for a long while as Dawad Kassis walked west on the beach, became a small dot in the distance, until he was gone.

www.ingramcontent.com/pod-product-compliance
Lightning Source LLC
Chambersburg PA
CBHW071824190726
48292CB00005B/1597

* 9 7 8 1 9 4 4 9 0 6 2 4 5 *